Singapore MATH PRACTICE

LEVEL 6A

Appropriate for Students in GRADE 7

Thinking Kids®
An imprint of Carson-Dellosa Publishing LLC
Greensboro, North Carolina

Visit carsondellosa.com for correlations to Common Core, state, national, and Canadian provincial standards.

Copyright © 2009 Singapore Asia Publishers PTE LTD.

Thinking Kids®
An imprint of Carson-Dellosa Publishing LLC
PO Box 35665
Greensboro, NC 27425 USA

ISBN 978-0-7682-3996-6
10-252197784

INTRODUCTION TO SINGAPORE MATH

Welcome to Singapore Math! The math curriculum in Singapore has been recognized worldwide for its excellence in producing students highly skilled in mathematics. Students in Singapore have ranked at the top in the world in mathematics on the *Trends in International Mathematics and Science Study* (TIMSS) in 1993, 1995, 2003, and 2008. Because of this, Singapore Math has gained in interest and popularity in the United States.

Singapore Math curriculum aims to help students develop the necessary math concepts and process skills for everyday life and to provide students with the ability to formulate, apply, and solve problems. Mathematics in the Singapore Primary (Elementary) Curriculum cover fewer topics but in greater depth. Key math concepts are introduced and built-on to reinforce various mathematical ideas and thinking. Students in Singapore are typically one grade level ahead of students in the United States.

The following pages provide examples of the various math problem types and skill sets taught in Singapore.

At an elementary level, some simple mathematical skills can help students understand mathematical principles. These skills are the counting-on, counting-back, and crossing-out methods. Note that these methods are most useful when the numbers are small.

1. The Counting-On Method

Used for addition of two numbers. Count on in 1s with the help of a picture or number line.

$$7 + 4 = 11$$

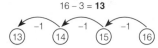

2. The Counting-Back Method

Used for subtraction of two numbers. Count back in 1s with the help of a picture or number line.

$$16 - 3 = 13$$

3. The Crossing-Out Method

Used for subtraction of two numbers. Cross out the number of items to be taken away. Count the remaining ones to find the answer.

$$20 - 12 = 8$$

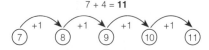

A **number bond** shows the relationship in a simple addition or subtraction problem. The number bond is based on the concept "part-part-whole." This concept is useful in teaching simple addition and subtraction to young children.

To find a whole, students must add the two parts.
To find a part, students must subtract the other part from the whole.

The different types of number bonds are illustrated below.

1. Number Bond (single digits)

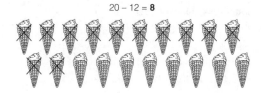

3 (part) + 6 (part) = **9** (whole)

9 (whole) − 3 (part) = **6** (part)

9 (whole) − 6 (part) = **3** (part)

2. Addition Number Bond (single digits)

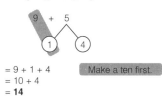

= 9 + 1 + 4

= 10 + 4

= **14**

Make a ten first.

3. Addition Number Bond (double and single digits)

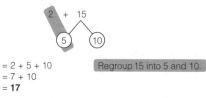

= 2 + 5 + 10

= 7 + 10

= **17**

Regroup 15 into 5 and 10.

4. Subtraction Number Bond (double and single digits)

$$12 - 7$$

10 − 7 = 3

3 + 2 = **5**

5. Subtraction Number Bond (double digits)

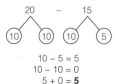

$$20 - 15$$

10 − 5 = 5

10 − 10 = 0

5 + 0 = **5**

Students should understand that multiplication is repeated addition and that division is the grouping of all items into equal sets.

1. Repeated Addition (Multiplication)

Mackenzie eats 2 rolls a day. How many rolls does she eat in 5 days?

$$2 + 2 + 2 + 2 + 2 = 10$$
$$5 \times 2 = 10$$

She eats **10** rolls in 5 days.

2. The Grouping Method (Division)

Mrs. Lee makes 14 sandwiches. She gives all the sandwiches equally to 7 friends. How many sandwiches does each friend receive?

$$14 \div 7 = 2$$

Each friend receives **2** sandwiches.

One of the basic but essential math skills students should acquire is to perform the 4 operations of whole numbers and fractions. Each of these methods is illustrated below.

1. The Adding-Without-Regrouping Method

H	T	O	
3	2	1	O: Ones
+ 5	6	8	T: Tens
8	**8**	**9**	H: Hundreds

Since no regrouping is required, add the digits in each place value accordingly.

2. The Adding-by-Regrouping Method

H	T	O	
¹4	9	2	O: Ones
+ 1	5	3	T: Tens
6	**4**	**5**	H: Hundreds

In this example, regroup 14 tens into 1 hundred 4 tens.

3. The Adding-by-Regrouping-Twice Method

```
  H  T  O
  ¹2 ¹8 6
+    3  6  5
─────────────
  6  5  1
```

O: Ones
T: Tens
H: Hundreds

Regroup twice in this example.
First, regroup 11 ones into 1 ten 1 one.
Second, regroup 15 tens into 1 hundred 5 tens.

4. The Subtracting-Without-Regrouping Method

```
  H  T  O
  7  3  9
−  3  2  5
─────────────
  4  1  4
```

O: Ones
T: Tens
H: Hundreds

Since no regrouping is required, subtract the digits in each place value accordingly.

5. The Subtracting-by-Regrouping Method

```
  H   T   O
  5  ⁷8 ¹¹1
−  2   4   7
─────────────
  3   3   4
```

O: Ones
T: Tens
H: Hundreds

In this example, students cannot subtract 7 ones from 1 one. So, regroup the tens and ones. Regroup 8 tens 1 one into 7 tens 11 ones.

6. The Subtracting-by-Regrouping-Twice Method

```
   H    T    O
  ⁷8  ⁹0  ¹⁰0
−  5    9    3
──────────────
   2    0    7
```

O: Ones
T: Tens
H: Hundreds

In this example, students cannot subtract 3 ones from 0 ones and 9 tens from 0 tens. So, regroup the hundreds, tens, and ones. Regroup 8 hundreds into 7 hundreds 9 tens 10 ones.

7. The Multiplying-Without-Regrouping Method

```
   T  O
   2  4
×     2
─────────
   4  8
```

O: Ones
T: Tens

Since no regrouping is required, multiply the digit in each place value by the multiplier accordingly.

8. The Multiplying-With-Regrouping Method

```
   H   T   O
  ¹3  ²4   9
×         3
─────────────
  1, 0  4  7
```

O: Ones
T: Tens
H: Hundreds

In this example, regroup 27 ones into 2 tens 7 ones, and 14 tens into 1 hundred 4 tens.

9. The Dividing-Without-Regrouping Method

```
        2 4 1
    2 ) 4 8 2
       −4
       ──
        8
       −8
       ──
        2
       −2
       ──
        0
```

Since no regrouping is required, divide the digit in each place value by the divisor accordingly.

10. The Dividing-With-Regrouping Method

```
        1 6 6
    5 ) 8 3 0
       −5
       ──
        3 3
       −3 0
       ───
          3 0
         −3 0
         ───
            0
```

In this example, regroup 3 hundreds into 30 tens and add 3 tens to make 33 tens. Regroup 3 tens into 30 ones.

11. The Addition-of-Fractions Method

$$\frac{1 \times 2}{6 \times 2} + \frac{1 \times 3}{4 \times 3} = \frac{2}{12} + \frac{3}{12} = \mathbf{\frac{5}{12}}$$

Always remember to make the denominators common before adding the fractions.

12. The Subtraction-of-Fractions Method

$$\frac{1 \times 5}{2 \times 5} - \frac{1 \times 2}{5 \times 2} = \frac{5}{10} - \frac{2}{10} = \mathbf{\frac{3}{10}}$$

Always remembers to make the denominators common before subtracting the fractions.

13. The Multiplication-of-Fractions Method

$$\frac{{}^1\cancel{3}}{5} \times \frac{1}{{}_3\cancel{9}} = \mathbf{\frac{1}{15}}$$

When the numerator and the denominator have a common multiple, reduce them to their lowest fractions.

14. The Division-of-Fractions Method

$$\frac{7}{9} \div \frac{1}{6} = \frac{7}{{}_3\cancel{9}} \times \frac{\cancel{6}^2}{1} = \frac{14}{3} = \mathbf{4\frac{2}{3}}$$

When dividing fractions, first change the division sign (÷) to the multiplication sign (×). Then, switch the numerator and denominator of the fraction on the right hand side. Multiply the fractions in the usual way.

Model drawing is an effective strategy used to solve math word problems. It is a visual representation of the information in word problems using bar units. By drawing the models, students will know of the variables given in the problem, the variables to find, and even the methods used to solve the problem.

Drawing models is also a versatile strategy. It can be applied to simple word problems involving addition, subtraction, multiplication, and division. It can also be applied to word problems related to fractions, decimals, percentage, and ratio.

The use of models also trains students to think in an algebraic manner, which uses symbols for representation.

The different types of bar models used to solve word problems are illustrated below.

1. The model that involves addition

Melissa has 50 blue beads and 20 red beads. How many beads does she have altogether?

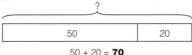

$50 + 20 = \mathbf{70}$

2. The model that involves subtraction

Ben and Andy have 90 toy cars. Andy has 60 toy cars. How many toy cars does Ben have?

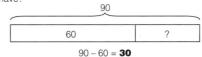

$90 − 60 = \mathbf{30}$

3. The model that involves comparison

Mr. Simons has 150 magazines and 110 books in his study. How many more magazines than books does he have?

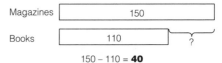

$150 − 110 = \mathbf{40}$

4. The model that involves two items with a difference

A pair of shoes costs $109. A leather bag costs $241 more than the pair of shoes. How much is the leather bag?

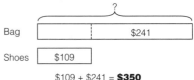

$109 + $241 = \mathbf{$350}$

5. The model that involves multiples

Mrs. Drew buys 12 apples. She buys 3 times as many oranges as apples. She also buys 3 times as many cherries as oranges. How many pieces of fruit does she buy altogether?

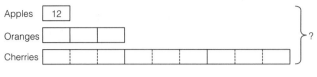

$$13 \times 12 = \textbf{156}$$

6. The model that involves multiples and difference

There are 15 students in Class A. There are 5 more students in Class B than in Class A. There are 3 times as many students in Class C than in Class A. How many students are there altogether in the three classes?

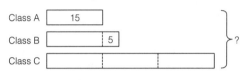

$$(5 \times 15) + 5 = \textbf{80}$$

7. The model that involves creating a whole

Ellen, Giselle, and Brenda bake 111 muffins. Giselle bakes twice as many muffins as Brenda. Ellen bakes 9 fewer muffins than Giselle. How many muffins does Ellen bake?

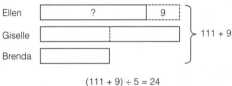

$$(111 + 9) \div 5 = 24$$
$$(2 \times 24) - 9 = \textbf{39}$$

8. The model that involves sharing

There are 183 tennis balls in Basket A and 97 tennis balls in Basket B. How many tennis balls must be transferred from Basket A to Basket B so that both baskets contain the same number of tennis balls?

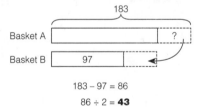

$$183 - 97 = 86$$
$$86 \div 2 = \textbf{43}$$

9. The model that involves fractions

George had 355 marbles. He lost $\frac{1}{5}$ of the marbles and gave $\frac{1}{4}$ of the remaining marbles to his brother. How many marbles did he have left?

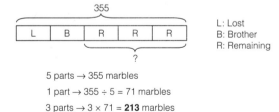

L: Lost
B: Brother
R: Remaining

5 parts → 355 marbles
1 part → 355 ÷ 5 = 71 marbles
3 parts → 3 × 71 = **213** marbles

10. The model that involves ratio

Aaron buys a tie and a belt. The prices of the tie and belt are in the ratio 2 : 5. If both items cost $539,

(a) what is the price of the tie?

(b) what is the price of the belt?

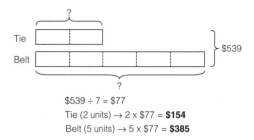

$539 ÷ 7 = $77
Tie (2 units) → 2 x $77 = **$154**
Belt (5 units) → 5 x $77 = **$385**

11. The model that involves comparison of fractions

Jack's height is $\frac{2}{3}$ of Leslie's height. Leslie's height is $\frac{3}{4}$ of Lindsay's height. If Lindsay is 160 cm tall, find Jack's height and Leslie's height.

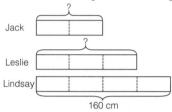

1 unit → 160 ÷ 4 = 40 cm

Leslie's height (3 units) → 3 × 40 = **120 cm**

Jack's height (2 units) → 2 × 40 = **80 cm**

Thinking skills and strategies are important in mathematical problem solving. These skills are applied when students think through the math problems to solve them. Below are some commonly used thinking skills and strategies applied in mathematical problem solving.

1. Comparing

Comparing is a form of thinking skill that students can apply to identify similarities and differences.

When comparing numbers, look carefully at each digit before deciding if a number is greater or less than the other. Students might also use a number line for comparison when there are more numbers.

Example:

3 is greater than 2 but smaller than 7.

2. Sequencing

A sequence shows the order of a series of numbers. *Sequencing* is a form of thinking skill that requires students to place numbers in a particular order. There are many terms in a sequence. The terms refer to the numbers in a sequence.

To place numbers in a correct order, students must first find a rule that generates the sequence. In a simple math sequence, students can either add or subtract to find the unknown terms in the sequence.

Example: Find the 7th term in the sequence below.

1,	4,	7,	10,	13,	16	?
1st term	2nd term	3rd term	4th term	5th term	6th term	7th term

Step 1:   This sequence is in an increasing order.

Step 2:   4 − 1 = 3   7 − 4 = 3
          The difference between two consecutive terms is 3.

Step 3:   16 + 3 = 19
          The 7th term is **19**.

3. Visualization

Visualization is a problem solving strategy that can help students visualize a problem through the use of physical objects. Students will play a more active role in solving the problem by manipulating these objects.

The main advantage of using this strategy is the mobility of information in the process of solving the problem. When students make a wrong step in the process, they can retrace the step without erasing or canceling it.

The other advantage is that this strategy helps develop a better understanding of the problem or solution through visual objects or images. In this way, students will be better able to remember how to solve these types of problems.

5

Some of the commonly used objects for this strategy are toothpicks, straws, cards, strings, water, sand, pencils, paper, and dice.

4. Look for a Pattern

This strategy requires the use of observational and analytical skills. Students have to observe the given data to find a pattern in order to solve the problem. Math word problems that involve the use of this strategy usually have repeated numbers or patterns.

Example: Find the sum of all the numbers from 1 to 100.

Step 1: Simplify the problem.
Find the sum of 1, 2, 3, 4, 5, 6, 7, 8, 9, and 10.

Step 2: Look for a pattern.

$1 + 10 = 11$	$2 + 9 = 11$	$3 + 8 = 11$
$4 + 7 = 11$	$5 + 6 = 11$	

Step 3: Describe the pattern.
When finding the sum of 1 to 10, add the first and last numbers to get a result of 11. Then, add the second and second last numbers to get the same result. The pattern continues until all the numbers from 1 to 10 are added. There will be 5 pairs of such results. Since each addition equals 11, the answer is then $5 \times 11 = 55$.

Step 4: Use the pattern to find the answer.
Since there are 5 pairs in the sum of 1 to 10, there should be ($10 \times 5 = 50$ pairs) in the sum of 1 to 100.

Note that the addition for each pair is not equal to 11 now. The addition for each pair is now ($1 + 100 = 101$).
$$50 \times 101 = 5050$$
The sum of all the numbers from 1 to 100 is **5,050**.

5. Working Backward

The strategy of working backward applies only to a specific type of math word problem. These word problems state the end result, and students are required to find the total number. In order to solve these word problems, students have to work backward by thinking through the correct sequence of events. The strategy of working backward allows students to use their logical reasoning and sequencing to find the answers.

Example: Sarah has a piece of ribbon. She cuts the ribbon into 4 equal parts. Each part is then cut into 3 smaller equal parts. If the length of each small part is 35 cm, how long is the piece of ribbon?
$$3 \times 35 = 105 \text{ cm}$$
$$4 \times 105 = 420 \text{ cm}$$
The piece of ribbon is **420 cm**.

6. The Before-After Concept

The *Before-After* concept lists all the relevant data before and after an event. Students can then compare the differences and eventually solve the problems. Usually, the Before-After concept and the mathematical model go hand in hand to solve math word problems. Note that the Before-After concept can be applied only to a certain type of math word problem, which trains students to think sequentially.

Example: Kelly has 4 times as much money as Joey. After Kelly uses some money to buy a tennis racquet, and Joey uses $30 to buy a pair of pants, Kelly has twice as much money as Joey. If Joey has $98 in the beginning,
(a) how much money does Kelly have in the end?
(b) how much money does Kelly spend on the tennis racquet?

Before

Kelly

Joey $98

After

Kelly

Joey $30

(a) $98 - $30 = $68
$2 \times $68 = 136
Kelly has **$136** in the end.

(b) $4 \times $98 = 392
$392 - $136 = 256
Kelly spends **$256** on the tennis racquet.

7. Making Supposition

Making supposition is commonly known as "making an assumption." Students can use this strategy to solve certain types of math word problems. Making assumptions will eliminate some possibilities and simplifies the word problems by providing a boundary of values to work within.

Example: Mrs. Jackson bought 100 pieces of candy for all the students in her class. How many pieces of candy would each student receive if there were 25 students in her class?

In the above word problem, assume that each student received the same number of pieces. This eliminates the possibilities that some students would receive more than others due to good behaviour, better results, or any other reason.

8. Representation of Problem

In problem solving, students often use representations in the solutions to show their understanding of the problems. Using representations also allow students to understand the mathematical concepts and relationships as well as to manipulate the information presented in the problems. Examples of representations are diagrams and lists or tables.

Diagrams allow students to consolidate or organize the information given in the problems. By drawing a diagram, students can see the problem clearly and solve it effectively.

A list or table can help students organize information that is useful for analysis. After analyzing, students can then see a pattern, which can be used to solve the problem.

9. Guess and Check

One of the most important and effective problem-solving techniques is *Guess and Check*. It is also known as *Trial and Error*. As the name suggests, students have to guess the answer to a problem and check if that guess is correct. If the guess is wrong, students will make another guess. This will continue until the guess is correct.

It is beneficial to keep a record of all the guesses and checks in a table. In addition, a *Comments* column can be included. This will enable students to analyze their guess (if it is too high or too low) and improve on the next guess. Be careful; this problem-solving technique can be tiresome without systematic or logical guesses.

Example: Jessica had 15 coins. Some of them were 10-cent coins and the rest were 5-cent coins. The total amount added up to $1.25. How many coins of each kind were there?

Use the guess-and-check method.

Number of 10¢ Coins	Value	Number of 5¢ Coins	Value	Total Number of Coins	Total Value
7	$7 \times 10¢ = 70¢$	8	$8 \times 5¢ = 40¢$	$7 + 8 = 15$	$70¢ + 40¢ = 110¢$ = $1.10
8	$8 \times 10¢ = 80¢$	7	$7 \times 5¢ = 35¢$	$8 + 7 = 15$	$80¢ + 35¢ = 115¢$ = $1.15
10	$10 \times 10¢ = 100¢$	5	$5 \times 5¢ = 25¢$	$10 + 5 = 15$	$100¢ + 25¢ = 125¢$ = $1.25

There were **ten** 10-cent coins and **five** 5-cent coins.

10. Restate the Problem

When solving challenging math problems, conventional methods may not be workable. Instead, restating the problem will enable students to see some challenging problems in a different light so that they can better understand them.

The strategy of restating the problem is to "say" the problem in a different and clearer way. However, students have to ensure that the main idea of the problem is not altered.

How do students restate a math problem?

First, read and understand the problem. Gather the given facts and unknowns. Note any condition(s) that have to be satisfied.

Next, restate the problem. Imagine narrating this problem to a friend. Present the given facts, unknown(s), and condition(s). Students may want to write the "revised" problem. Once the "revised" problem is analyzed, students should be able to think of an appropriate strategy to solve it.

11. Simplify the Problem

One of the commonly used strategies in mathematical problem solving is simplification of the problem. When a problem is simplified, it can be "broken down" into two or more smaller parts. Students can then solve the parts systematically to get to the final answer.

Singapore Math Practice Level 6A

Table of Contents

Singapore Math Practice Level 6A

LEARNING OUTCOMES

Unit 1 Algebra

Students should be able to

- ✖ use a letter to denote an unknown number.
- ✖ simplify an algebraic expression.
- ✖ solve an algebraic expression using the method of substitution.
- ✖ solve story problems related to algebra.

Unit 2 Angles

Students should be able to

- ✖ calculate unknown angles in geometric figures like a square, rectangle, parallelogram, rhombus, trapezium, and different types of triangles.

Review 1

This review tests students' understanding of Units 1 & 2.

Unit 3 Identifying Solids and Nets

Students should be able to

- ✖ identify different types of solids.
- ✖ identify the faces of a cube, cuboid, prism, and pyramid.
- ✖ state the number of faces of a cube, cuboid, prism, and pyramid.
- ✖ identify the nets of a solid such as cube, cuboid, prism, and pyramid.
- ✖ recognize a solid based on its net.

Unit 4 Fractions

Students should be able to

- ✖ perform four operations of fractions.
- ✖ divide a whole number by a proper fraction.
- ✖ divide a proper fraction by a proper fraction.
- ✖ solve story problems related to fractions.

Review 2

This review tests students' understanding of Units 3 & 4.

Unit 5 Ratio

Students should be able to

- ✖ express a fraction as a ratio and vice versa.
- ✖ express 2 quantities as a fraction.
- ✖ find the number of times one quantity is as large as another in terms of ratio and vice versa.
- ✖ compare ratios.
- ✖ solve story problems related to ratios.

Unit 6 Percentage

Students should be able to

- ✖ express a fraction as a percentage and vice versa.
- ✖ express a decimal as a percentage and vice versa.
- ✖ find the whole when a part and the percentage are given.
- ✖ find a part when the whole and percentage of another part are given.
- ✖ find percentage increase and decrease.
- ✖ solve story problems related to percentage, discount, sales tax, percentage increase, and percentage decrease.

Revision 3

This review tests students' understanding of Units 5 & 6.

Final Review

This review is an excellent assessment of students' understanding of all the topics learned in this series.

Singapore Math Practice Level 6A

FORMULA SHEET

Unit 1 Algebra

Lowercase letters are used to represent unknown numbers in algebra.

Example: Mr. Johnson has x watches in his collection.

An **algebraic expression** includes a letter, an arithmetic operator, and a number.

Examples: $x + 3$, $7 - b$, $5n$, $\frac{y}{9}$

Evaluating an algebraic expression

When the value of a letter is known, substitute it into the algebraic expression to get the answer.

Example: Find the value of $23z + 39$ when $z = 7$.
$$23z + 39 = 23 \times 7 + 39 = 200$$

Simplifying an algebraic expression

1. Group the algebra together.
   Keep in mind the arithmetic operators $(+, -, \times, \div)$ in front of each variable. When the variable has to be moved, that arithmetic operator will follow.
2. Perform the arithmetic operation as usual.

Example: Simplify $6x + 20 + 3x - 15$.
$$6x + 20 + 3x - 15 = 6x + 3x + 20 - 15 = 9x + 5$$

Unit 2 Angles

The properties of angles are summarized below.

Diagram	Property of angle
115° 65°	The sum of angles on a straight line is 180°.
130° 95° 90° 45°	The sum of angles at a point is 360°.
105° 38° 37°	The sum of angles in a triangle is 180°.
125° 55° 55° 125°	Vertically opposite angles are equal.
45° 90° 45°	An isosceles triangle has two equal sides and two equal angles.
60° 60° 60°	An equilateral triangle has three equal sides and three equal angles.
124° 56° 56° 124°	Angles between two parallel lines are 180°.
124° 56° 56° 124°	Opposite angles are equal.

Unit 3 Identifying Solids and Nets

Solid	Number of faces	Shape(s) of face	Example of net
cube	6	square	
cuboid	6	rectangle	
cuboid	6	square rectangle	
prism	5	rectangle triangle	
pyramid	4	triangle	
pyramid	5	triangle square	
pyramid	5	triangle rectangle	

Unit 4 Fractions

Adding fractions

1. Make sure the denominators of all fractions are common.
2. Add the numerators.
3. Reduce to its simplest form if required.

Example: $\frac{2}{5} + \frac{1}{10} = \frac{4}{10} + \frac{1}{10} = \frac{5}{10} = \frac{1}{2}$

Subtracting fractions

1. Make sure the denominators of all fractions are common.
2. Subtract the numerators.
3. Reduce to its simplest form if required.

Example: $\frac{1}{2} - \frac{3}{12} = \frac{6}{12} - \frac{3}{12} = \frac{3}{12} = \frac{1}{4}$

Multiplying fractions

1. Multiply both numerators.
2. Multiply both denominators.
3. Reduce to its simplest form if required.

Singapore Math Practice Level 6A

Alternatively, use the cancellation method.
When there is a common factor between the numerator of one fraction and the denominator of another, "cancel" them by reducing both to their lowest factor.

Example: $\dfrac{\overset{1}{\cancel{5}}}{\underset{4}{\cancel{12}}} \times \dfrac{\overset{1}{\cancel{3}}}{\underset{2}{\cancel{10}}} = \dfrac{1 \times 1}{4 \times 2} = \dfrac{1}{8}$

<u>Dividing a whole number by a proper fraction</u>
1. Change the division sign ($\div$) to a multiplication sign ($\times$).
2. Find the reciprocal of the proper fraction by interchanging its numerator and denominator.
3. Multiply the numerators.
4. Multiply the denominators.
5. Reduce to its simplest form if required.

Example: $3 \div \dfrac{1}{2} = 3 \times \dfrac{2}{1} = \dfrac{6}{1} = 6$

<u>Dividing a proper fraction by a proper fraction</u>
1. Change the division sign ($\div$) to a multiplication sign ($\times$).
2. Find the reciprocal of the proper fraction on the right-hand side by interchanging its numerator and denominator.
3. Multiply the numerators.
4. Multiply the denominators.
5. Reduce to its simplest form if required.

Example: $\dfrac{1}{4} \div \dfrac{1}{8} = \dfrac{1}{4} \times \dfrac{8}{1} = \dfrac{8}{4} = 2$

Unit 5 Ratio
<u>Ratio and Fraction</u>
Write a ratio as a fraction.

Example: When A is $\dfrac{2}{3}$ of B,

$$\begin{array}{cc} A & : & B \\ 2 & : & 3 \end{array}$$

Similarly, a fraction can be written as a ratio.

Example: The ratio of A to B is 6 : 7.

A is $\dfrac{6}{7}$ of B, and B is $\dfrac{7}{6}$ of A.

<u>Comparing ratio</u>
When one quantity in a ratio increases, the other quantity increases by the same multiplier. In order to find the unknown in a ratio, find the multiplier.

Example:
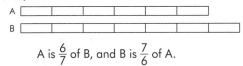

Unit 6 Percentage
<u>Percentage and Fraction</u>
When expressing percentage as a fraction,
1. the denominator of the fraction must be 100,
2. reduce to its simplest form if required.

Example: Write 35% as a fraction.

$$35\% = \dfrac{35}{100} = \dfrac{7}{20}$$

When writing a fraction as a percentage,
1. make the denominator of the fraction 100,
2. multiply the numerator of the fraction by the same multiplier.

Example: Express $\dfrac{6}{20}$ as a percentage.

$$\dfrac{6 \times 5}{20 \times 5} = \dfrac{30}{100} = 30\%$$

<u>Percentage and Decimal</u>
When expressing a decimal as a percentage, multiply the decimal by 100%.

Example: Express 0.16 as a percentage.
$$0.16 = 0.16 \times 100\% = 16\%$$

When expressing a percentage as a decimal, divide the percentage by 100%.

Example: Write 89% as a decimal.
$$89\% = 89 \div 100 = 0.89$$

<u>Percentage increase</u>
Amount of increase = increased amount – original amount

Amount of increase = $\dfrac{\text{increase (in \%)}}{100\%} \times$ original amount

Percentage increase = $\dfrac{\text{amount of increase}}{\text{original amount}} \times 100\%$

<u>Percentage decrease</u>
Amount of decrease = original amount – decreased amount

Amount of decrease = $\dfrac{\text{decrease (in \%)}}{100\%} \times$ original amount

Percentage decrease = $\dfrac{\text{amount of decrease}}{\text{original amount}} \times 100\%$

<u>Discount</u>
Amount of discount = usual price – selling price

Amount of discount = $\dfrac{\text{discount (in \%)}}{100\%} \times$ original amount

Percentage discount = $\dfrac{\text{amount of discount}}{\text{original amount}} \times 100\%$

<u>Tax</u>
Amount of tax = final price – price before tax

Amount of tax = $\dfrac{\text{tax (in \%)}}{100\%} \times$ price before tax

tax percentage = $\dfrac{\text{amount of tax}}{\text{price before tax}} \times 100\%$

<u>Interest</u>
Amount of interest = amount with profit – principal amount

Amount of interest = $\dfrac{\text{interest (in \%)}}{100\%} \times$ principal amount

Interest percentage = $\dfrac{\text{amount of interest}}{\text{principal amount}} \times 100\%$

Unit 1: ALGEBRA

Give an expression for each of the following. Write your answers on the lines.

1. Mrs. Cole bought x pencils. She distributed the pencils among 40 students. How many pencils did each student receive?

    $x \div 40 =$ $\underline{x \div 40}$

2. Jessica buys 10 similar dresses. Each dress costs $\$y$. How much must she pay in all?

                                                                     $\underline{y \cdot 10}$

Singapore Math Practice Level 6A

3. Ping was *m* years old 2 years ago. How old will he be this year?

$m + 2$

4. Sisay bought *z* apples. She gave 5 apples to her friends. How many apples did she have left?

$z - 5$

5. Marta got 88 points on her English test. Sandy got *x* points on the same test. What was their average score?

$(88 + x) \div 2$

6. Gordon has *n* stamps. Ahmed has twice as many stamps as Gordon. Peter has three times as many stamps as Ahmed. How many stamps does Peter have?

$2n \times 3$

7. Mey had $50. She gave half of the money to her sister. Her mother gave Mey $*a*. How much money did Mey have in the end?

$(50 \div 2) + a$

8. Joy has *x* balloons. Maggie has *y* balloons. Helen has *z* balloons. How many balloons do they have in all?

$x + y + z$

9. Miriam baked *z* cakes. She gave 5 cakes to her neighbors and 12 cakes to her relatives. How many cakes did she have left?

$(z - 5) - 12$

10. Felicia's boat consumed *x* gallons of gasoline on Monday. It consumed twice the amount of gasoline on Tuesday. How much gasoline was left if Felicia pumped 50 gallons of gasoline before Monday?

$2x + 50$

Singapore Math Practice Level 6A

Evaluate the following algebraic expressions when y = 6.

11. $1 + y + 9 = $ _16_

12. $y - 3 + 2 = $ _5_

13. $y + y + y = $ _18_

14. $2y = $ _12_

15. $y^2 = $ _36_

16. $\dfrac{y}{2} = $ _3_

17. $3y + 2y = $ _30_

18. $8y \div 12 = $ _4_

19. $3y + 4y - 3 = $ _39_

20. $10y - 4y + 21 - 13 = $ _44_
    60 24 &
        37

Simplify the following algebraic expressions.

21. $a + a + 2a = $ _4a_

22. $5b - 3b + 6b = $ _8b_

23. $3c + 2c - 4c = $ _1c_

24. $6d - d - 2d = $ _3d_

25. $4 + 2e + 5 = $ _9 + 2e_

26. $9 + 5 + f + 4f = $ _14 + 5f_

27. $4g - 2g - 3 = $ _2g - 3_

28. $7h + 4 - 5h - h = $ _13h + 4_

29. $3x - 6 - x = $ _4x - 6_

30. $10 + 10k + 3 + 14k = $ _24k + 10_

Write your answers on the lines. You may use a calculator whenever you see .

31. $18a = 6 \times \boxed{3a}$. What is the missing value? _____

32. Ally bought 10 books which cost $2m each. If she gave the cashier a fifty dollar bill, how much change would she receive?

    (50 - (10 · 2m)

33. If b = 12, find the perimeter of a rectangle with a length of 3b cm and a width of 10 cm.

    360

Singapore Math Practice Level 6A

34. The length of a square is 7a in. Find its area if a = 2.

_196_

35. If a = 7 and b = 10, find the value of a + 3b × 2 – b.

30 10
60
67

_57_

36. If 14a = 84, what will a + 10 be?

_616_

37. Find the value of 4x – 2x if x = 3.

_6_

38. $\frac{1}{2}$ of n = 14. What is n?

_28_

39. Subtract 3k from the product of 9 and 2k. What is the answer?

_15k_

40. LaToya had $(10y + 6). She bought a dress which cost $3y and a pair of shoes which cost twice as much as the dress. How much money did Latoya have left?

Solve the following story problems. Show your work in the space below.

41. The parking charges at a shopping center were $2 for the first hour and $d for every hour or part of an hour after that. Calvin parked his car at the shopping center from 2:30 P.M. to 5:10 P.M. How much did he have to pay for parking? Write your answer in terms of d.

$(3 + 2d) + 2 =$

16

42. Judi has 80 pieces of candy and Wendy has x pieces of candy fewer than Judi.

   (a) How many pieces must Judi give to Wendy so that both will have an equal number? Write your answer in terms of x.

   (b) If $x = 40$, how many pieces of candy do they have altogether?

$$\frac{x}{2}$$

$80 - x = 8$ $0 + 40 = 120$

Singapore Math Practice Level 6A

43. Fernando, Joyce, and Dawit received some marbles in the ratio 6 : 5 : 3. If Fernando received 18y marbles,

   (a) find the number of marbles Joyce received in terms of y.

   (b) find the total number of marbles the three children had in terms of y.

15y

24

42y

44. A rectangular tank 18 cm long and 12 cm wide was filled with water to a height of y cm. The water level increased to 10 cm when some marbles were placed into the tank.

(a) What was the increase in the water level in terms of y?

(b) If $y = 8$ cm, find the increase in volume of water after the marbles were placed into the tank.

Singapore Math Practice Level 6A

45. After spending $b, Miss Kazuo found that she still had $125 left.

 (a) How much money did Miss Kazuo have in the beginning? Write your answer in terms of b.

 (b) If $b = 75$, how much money did Miss Kazuo have in the beginning?

46. At a fast food restaurant, a milk shake costs $r. A chicken sandwich costs 3 times as much as the shake. A large order of French fries costs $3.

(a) Find the total cost of a shake and a chicken sandwich. Write your answer in terms of r.

(b) If $r = 2$, how much do 3 chicken sandwiches and 2 large orders of French fries cost?

47. A box of 6 forks cost $y. Olivia bought 5 boxes of forks.

    (a) Find the cost of each fork in terms of y.

    (b) If y = 18, how much did Olivia pay for 5 boxes of forks?

48. There were x children and half as many adults as children at a library in the morning. An hour later, three times the number of children and 40 adults visited the library.

(a) How many people were at the library altogether?

(b) If x = 56, find the total number of people at the library.

Singapore Math Practice Level 6A

Unit 2: ANGLES

Examples:

1. ABCD is a rhombus. ABD is an equilateral triangle. ∠BAD = 60°. Find ∠ABC and ∠DCB.

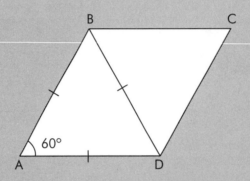

$\angle$ABC = 180° – 60° = **120°** (∠s between two parallel lines = 180°)

$\angle$DCB = **60°**   (opposite ∠s are equal)

2. TUVW is a square. STU is an isosceles triangle where ST = TU. Find ∠SUV.

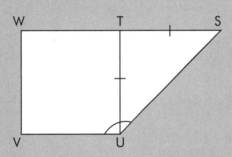

$\angle$UTW = $\angle$TUV = 90°   (right ∠ in a square)

$\angle$STU = 180° – 90° = 90°   (∠s on a straight line)

$\angle$TSU = $\angle$SUT = $\dfrac{180° - 90°}{2}$ = 45°   (isosceles Δ)

$\angle$SUV = 90° + 45° = **135°**

Singapore Math Practice Level 6A

These figures are not drawn to scale. Find the unknown angles.

1. ABC is an isosceles triangle where AB = BC. Find ∠ABC.

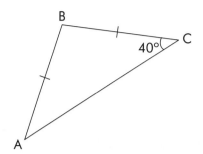

_____

2. AOB is a straight line. Find ∠DOB.

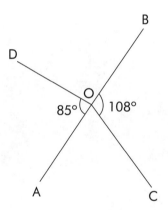

_____

3. AOB is a straight line. Find ∠COD.

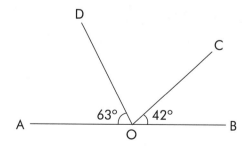

_____

Singapore Math Practice Level 6A

4. ACB is a triangle. ABD is a straight line. Find ∠CBD.

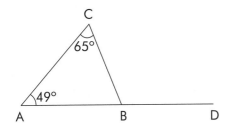

_____

5. PRQ is an isosceles triangle where PQ = QR. PQS is a straight line. Find ∠PRQ.

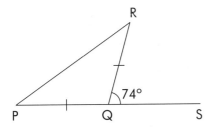

_____

6. WZYX is a trapezoid where WX // ZY. Find ∠WZY.

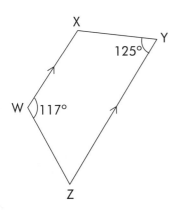

_____

7. ABCD is a rhombus. ABE is a straight line. Find ∠ADC.

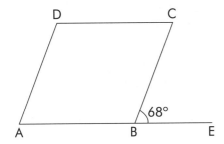

_____

8. PQRS is a parallelogram. Find ∠SRQ.

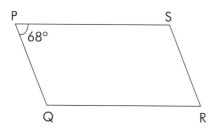

_____

9. ABC is a triangle. ACD and BCE are straight lines. Find ∠DCE.

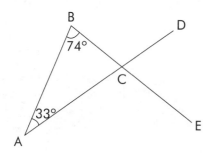

_____

10. XYZ is an equilateral triangle. XZW is a straight line. Find ∠YZW.

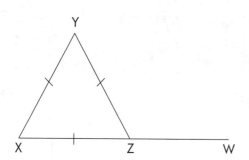

_____

11. ACB is a triangle and ADB is a straight line. Find ∠ABC.

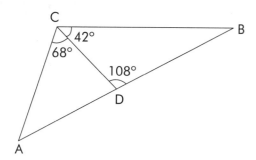

_____

27

Singapore Math Practice Level 6A

12. ABCD is a parallelogram. DCE is an isosceles triangle where DC = DE. BCE is a straight line. Find ∠ADC.

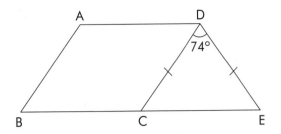

_____

13. PQRS is a trapezoid where PQ // SR. RST is a right triangle. PST is a straight line. Find ∠QRT.

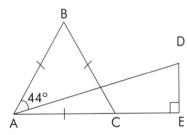

_____

14. ABC is an equilateral triangle and AED is a right triangle. ACE is a straight line. Find ∠EDA.

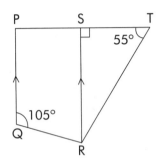

_____

15. WXYZ is a rhombus. Find ∠YXZ.

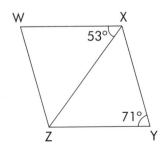

_____

Singapore Math Practice Level 6A

16. ABC is a right triangle. AZYX is a trapezoid where AX // ZY. AZB is a straight line. Find ∠ABC.

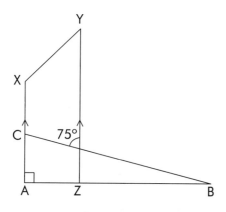

_____

17. ABCD is a trapezoid where AD // BC. CDEF is a rhombus. ADE and BCF are straight lines. Find ∠DEF.

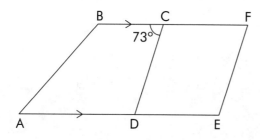

_____

18. ABCD is a rhombus. BCD is an isosceles triangle with BC = CD. EDC is a straight line. Find ∠ADB.

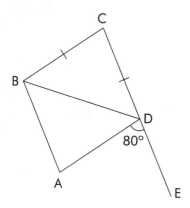

_____

Singapore Math Practice Level 6A

19. ABCD is a parallelogram and CDE is a triangle. ADF and BCE are straight lines. Find ∠FDE.

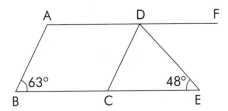

_____

20. ABCD is a square and AECF is a parallelogram. Find ∠FCD.

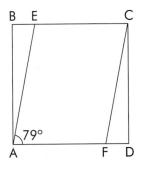

_____

Singapore Math Practice Level 6A

REVIEW 1

Choose the correct answer, and write its number in the parentheses.

1. Calculate $16a - 6a$ when $a = 3$.

   (1)   10   (3)   30

   (2)   18   (4)   48   (   )

2. Simplify $6a + 6 + 27a - 3$.

   (1) $33a$ (3) $33a - 9$

   (2) $33a + 3$ (4) $36a$ (   )

3. The figure is not drawn to scale. ABC is an equilateral triangle. BCDE is a trapezoid where BE // CD. ACD is a straight line. Find $\angle$CBE.

   (1)   60°

   (2)   90°

   (3)   120°

   (4)   150°

   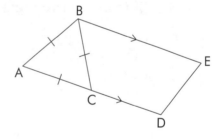

   (   )

4. The figure is not drawn to scale. PQRS is a parallelogram and STR is a triangle. Find $\angle$PTS.

   (1)   31°

   (2)   44°

   (3)   75°

   (4)   105°

   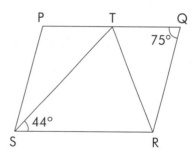

   (   )

5. Kate has *x* stickers. Stoya has 4 times as many stickers as Kate. Yui has 7 more stickers than Stoya. How many stickers does Yui have?

   (1) $x + 7$

   (2) $4x$

   (3) $4x + 7$

   (4) $28x$ (   )

6. The figure is not drawn to scale. WXYZ is a rhombus and UWX is a right triangle. Find $\angle$XUY.

   (1)   39°

   (2)   51°

   (3)   90°

   (4)   141°

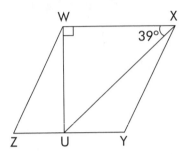
(   )

7. Cecilia had $z. She gave $23 to her brother. Her father gave her another $16. If z = 81, how much did Cecilia have in the end?

   (1) $39

   (2) $58

   (3) $74

   (4) $120   (   )

Write your answers on the lines. You may use a calculator whenever you see **.**

8. Simplify $5a + 9 + 7a - 3$.   _____

9. Linda is *b* years old. Her mother is 6 times as old as Linda. Her grandmother is 20 years older than her mother. Find Linda's grandmother's age.

10. The figure is not drawn to scale. ABED is a trapezoid where AD // BE. CDE is an isosceles triangle where DE = DC. Find $\angle$DAB.

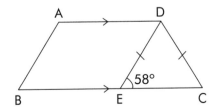

Singapore Math Practice Level 6A

11. Calculate the algebraic expression when $y = 13$.

$8y - 29 + 3y - 18$

_____

12. The figure is not drawn to scale. WXY is a right triangle and WYZ is a straight line. Find $\angle$WXY.

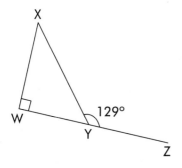

_____

13. The figure is not drawn to scale. ACB is an isosceles triangle where AC = AB. CAD is a triangle. CDE is a straight line. Find $\angle$DAB.

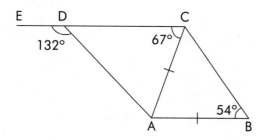

_____

14. The average mass of three boys is $6v$ kg. The average mass of two girls is $6v$ kg. Find the average mass of the five children.

_____

15. George bought a dozen pencils. The pencils cost $\$m$. What was the cost of each pencil?

_____

Singapore Math Practice Level 6A

Solve the following story problems. Show your work in the space below.

16. Rabi is $(n + 4)$ years old now. Edwin is 6 years old.

   (a)   What will be their total age in 10 years? Write your answer in terms of n.

   (b)   If $n = 8$, find their total age in 10 years.

17. The figure is not drawn to scale. ABCD is a trapezoid where AD // BC. CDE is a triangle. ADE is a straight line. Find ∠BCD.

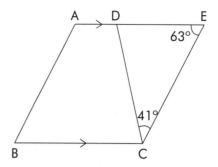

18. The figure is not drawn to scale. ABC is an equilateral triangle. BCD is an isosceles triangle where CD = CB. BCE and ACD are straight lines. Find ∠x.

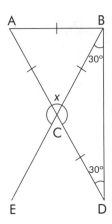

19. Patricia has m cards. Sachiko has 3 times as many cards as Patricia. Ivy has 22 more cards than Patricia while Casey has $(m + 12)$ more cards than Sachiko.

    (a)   How many cards do they have altogether? Write your answer in terms of m.

    (b)   If they share all the cards equally, how many cards does each girl get? Write your answer in terms of m.

20. Alicia bought a wallet for $29. She bought a purse which cost 5 times as much as the wallet.

   (a)   If Alicia had y left after buying these two items, how much did Alicia have in the beginning? Write your answer in terms of y.

   (b)   If $y = 52$, how much did Alicia have in the beginning?

Unit 3: IDENTIFYING SOLIDS AND NETS

Examples:

1. Identify this solid.

    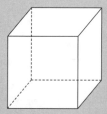

    This solid is a **cube**.

2. The net of a solid is shown below.

    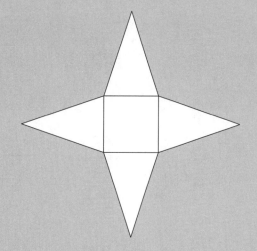

    (a) Identify the solid.   <u>pyramid</u>

    (b) How many faces does the solid have?   <u>5</u>

    (c) What are the shapes of faces?   <u>triangle and square</u>

Singapore Math Practice Level 6A

Look at each solid carefully. Write the shape on the lines.

cube	cuboid	prism	pyramid	cylinder	cone

1.
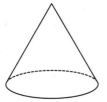

_____

2.
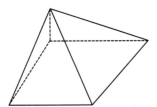

_____

3.
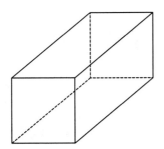

_____

4.

_____

Singapore Math Practice Level 6A

5.

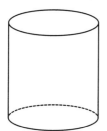

_____

6.

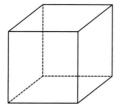

_____

For each solid, state the number of face(s) and identify the shape(s) of faces.

7.

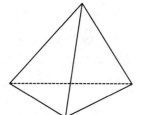

Number of faces: _____

Shape(s) of faces: _____

8.

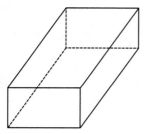

Number of faces: _____

Shape(s) of faces: _____

Singapore Math Practice Level 6A

9.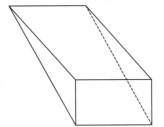

Number of faces: _____

Shape(s) of faces: _____

10.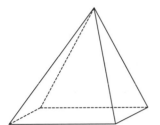

Number of faces: _____

Shape(s) of faces: _____

11.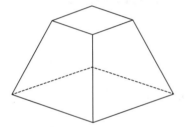

Number of faces: _____

Shape(s) of faces: _____

12.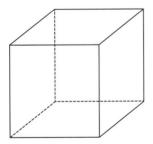

Number of faces: _____

Shape(s) of faces: _____

Singapore Math Practice Level 6A

The figure below shows a cube. Write *Yes* in the blank if it shows the correct net of the cube. Write *No* in the blank if it does not show the correct net of the cube.

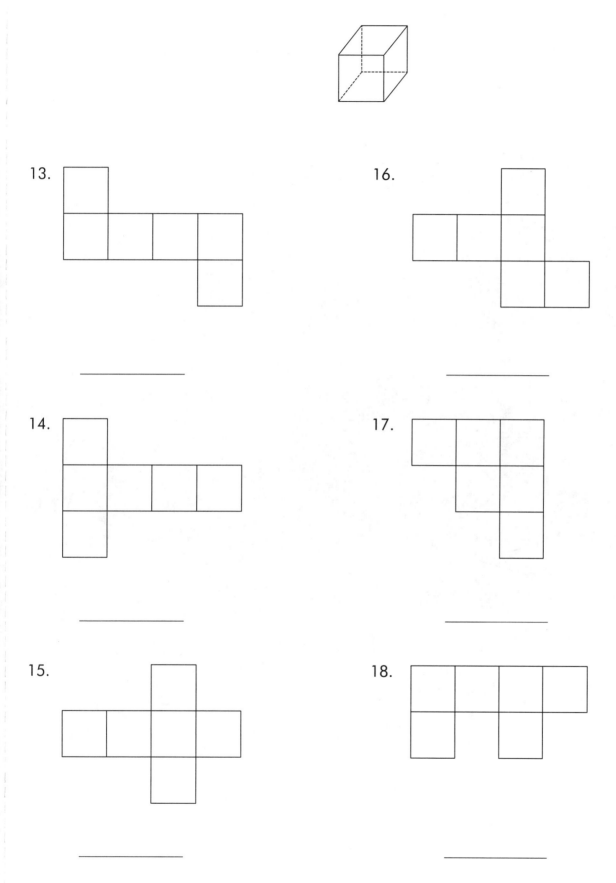

13. _____

14. _____

15. _____

16. _____

17. _____

18. _____

Match each net to the correct solid.

19.   •   •

20.   •   •

21.   •   •

22.   •   •

23.   •   •

Singapore Math Practice Level 6A

Unit 4: FRACTIONS

Examples:

1. A maid takes $\frac{3}{4}$ hr. to clean a hotel room. If she works nonstop for 6 hr., how many hotel rooms will she clean?

$$6 \div \frac{3}{4} = 6 \times \frac{4}{3} = 8$$

She will clean **8** hotel rooms.

2. After purchasing some books, Gisele had $\frac{1}{2}$ of her money left. She used the remaining money to purchase some magazines. If the cost of each magazine was $\frac{1}{6}$ of her money, how many magazines did Gisele buy?

$$\frac{1}{2} \div \frac{1}{6} = \frac{1}{2} \times 6 = 3$$

Gisele bought **3** magazines

Singapore Math Practice Level 6A

Find the value of each of the following. Write the correct answer in each blank.

1. $\dfrac{1}{7} + \dfrac{1}{2} =$ _____

2. $\dfrac{12}{9} \times \dfrac{3}{4} =$ _____

3. $\dfrac{2}{5} - \dfrac{1}{10} =$ _____

4. $\dfrac{3}{11} \div 6 =$ _____

5. $2\dfrac{1}{3} \times 8 =$ _____

6. $7\dfrac{1}{5} - 2\dfrac{2}{3} =$ _____

7. $10\dfrac{2}{9} + 15\dfrac{1}{8} =$ _____

8. $5\dfrac{1}{5} \div 3 =$ _____

9. $6 \div \dfrac{1}{3} =$ _____

10. $9 \div \dfrac{3}{5} =$ _____

11. $\dfrac{1}{7} \div \dfrac{1}{2} =$ _____

12. $\dfrac{4}{9} \div \dfrac{8}{11} =$ _____

13. $\dfrac{6}{7} \div \dfrac{2}{7} =$ _____

14. $36 \div \dfrac{8}{9} =$ _____

15. $\dfrac{3}{8} \div \dfrac{3}{4} =$ _____

Write your answers on the lines.

16. Janice used $\frac{2}{5}$ gal. of water to water a pot of flowers. She used $\frac{1}{8}$ gal. of water to wash her cup. How much water did she use to do these two tasks?

_____

17. 7 similar rooms were painted by a group of volunteers. Each volunteer painted $\frac{1}{4}$ of the room. How many volunteers were there?

_____

18. The mass of a bag of sugar is $\frac{7}{8}$ kg. Mrs. Wincheski uses $\frac{1}{8}$ kg of sugar to bake a cake. How many cakes can she bake?

_____

19. Christopher used $\frac{1}{3}$ of a day to sleep. He used $\frac{1}{5}$ of the day for recreation. The rest of the day was spent working on a project. What fraction of the day did he spend working on the project?

_____

20. Max had 3 pizzas. He shared the pizzas with his neighbors. Each of them ate $\frac{3}{7}$ of a pizza. How many people ate the pizzas?

_____

Singapore Math Practice Level 6A

Solve the following story problems. Show your work in the space below. You may use a calculator whenever you see ▧.

21. Miss Rivera is a piano teacher. She taught a total of 24 hours in the month of June. Each lesson lasted $\frac{3}{4}$ hr. How many lessons did she teach in the month of June?

Singapore Math Practice Level 6A

22. Fala made some brownies for a school fair. She sold $\frac{3}{5}$ of them and gave away 69 brownies. She had 23 brownies left. How many brownies did Fala make?

23. Aunt Mary spends $\frac{1}{5}$ of her household budget on groceries and $\frac{1}{2}$ of it on utilities. The rest of her household budget is spent on pet grooming.

(a) Each pet uses $\frac{1}{10}$ of her household budget. How many pets does Aunt Mary have?

(b) She spends $375 on pet grooming. How much is her household budget?

24. Mr. Lee bought a bag of snacks. $\frac{3}{4}$ of the snacks were yogurt bars, and the remaining snacks were chocolate bars. The snacks were distributed equally among his children. His sons would get the chocolate bars, while his daughters would get the yogurt bars. Each son got $\frac{1}{8}$ of the snacks, while each daughter got $\frac{1}{4}$ of the snacks.

   (a) How many sons and daughters does Mr. Lee have?

   (b) If each son got 3 chocolate bars and each daughter got 6 yogurt bars, how many snacks did Mr. Lee buy?

25. 92 teachers and students took part in a recycling exercise. $\frac{3}{4}$ of the participants were students. The teachers brought an equal number of empty soda cans each. All students brought the same number of empty soda cans. Each student brought $\frac{1}{5}$ as many empty soda cans as each teacher. The difference between the empty soda cans brought by the teachers and students was 138.

(a) How many teachers took part in the recycling exercise?

(b) How many empty soda cans did each student bring?

(c) How many empty soda cans were collected altogether?

Singapore Math Practice Level 6A

REVIEW 2

Choose the correct answer, and write its number in the parentheses.

1. The net of a figure is shown below. What is the figure?

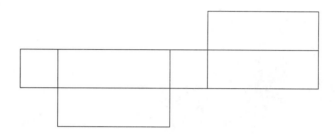

    (1)   cube   (3)   pyramid

    (2)   cone   (4)   cuboid   (   )

2. Find the value of $\frac{1}{7} \times \frac{8}{9}$.

    (1) $\frac{8}{56}$ (3) $\frac{47}{63}$

    (2) $\frac{8}{63}$ (4) $1\frac{2}{63}$ (   )

3. There are some sandwiches on the shelf. $\frac{1}{3}$ of them are egg sandwiches, and $\frac{1}{2}$ of them are club sandwiches. The rest are peanut butter sandwiches. What fraction of the sandwiches are peanut butter?

    (1) $\frac{1}{6}$ (3) $\frac{1}{2}$

    (2) $\frac{1}{4}$ (4) $\frac{5}{6}$ (   )

Singapore Math Practice Level 6A

4. Below shows the net of a solid. Which of the following solids can be formed by this net?

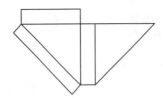

(1)

(3)

(2)

(4)

( )

5. Find the value of $\frac{3}{5} \div \frac{1}{10}$.

(1) $\frac{3}{50}$

(3) 5

(2) $\frac{1}{2}$

(4) 6

( )

6. Wendy brought 6 pies to her office. The pies were shared by a group of colleagues. If each colleague ate $\frac{1}{2}$ of a pie. How many colleagues shared the pies?

(1) 3

(3) 12

(2) 4

(4) 24

( )

7. Fiona had 3 lb. of spinach. $\frac{1}{2}$ lb. of spinach was sold to Mrs. Simon and the rest was packed equally into 3 bags. Find the mass of each bag of spinach.

(1) $\frac{1}{2}$ lb.

(3) 1 lb.

(2) $\frac{5}{6}$ lb.

(4) $2\frac{1}{2}$ lb.

( )

Write your answers on the lines. You may use a calculator whenever you see .

8. Figure X has 4 faces. All its faces are triangular. Identify Figure X.

_____

9. What is $9 \div \frac{3}{7}$?

_____

10. Jamie pours $\frac{3}{4}$ L of tea equally into 6 cups. How much tea is in each cup?

_____

11. Identify the shape(s) of the faces that this solid has.

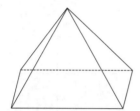

_____

12. Below shows the net of a solid. Identify the solid.

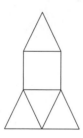

_____

13. An author wrote $\frac{1}{4}$ of a book in the first week and another $\frac{1}{8}$ of it in the second week. He finished writing the book in another two weeks. If he wrote 95 pages in the last two weeks, what was the total number of pages in the book?

_____

Singapore Math Practice Level 6A

14. A bag of apples has a mass of 4 kg. The average mass of each apple is $\frac{1}{8}$ kg. How many apples are in the bag?

_____

15. Zoe has some cloth. She uses the cloth to make 12 pillowcases. Each pillowcase uses $\frac{5}{8}$ yd. of the cloth. She still has $\frac{5}{12}$ yd. of cloth left. How long is the cloth?

_____

Solve the following story problems. Show your work in the space below.

16. Below shows the net of a solid.

    (a)   Find the number of faces that this solid has when its net is folded.

    (b)   State the shape(s) of the faces.

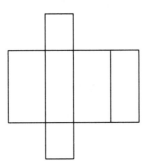

17. At a seminar, $\frac{2}{5}$ of the audience were students. $\frac{3}{10}$ of them were retirees. The rest were professionals. There were 18 more students than professionals. How many people were in the audience at the seminar?

18. 240 marbles were shared between some boys and 3 girls. The number of marbles that the girls had was $\frac{3}{8}$ of the total number of marbles.

(a)   Find the number of marbles each girl had.

(b)   If each boy had 25 marbles, how many boys were there?

Singapore Math Practice Level 6A

19. Below is a net of a figure. Identify the figure.

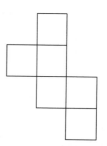

20. Sarah spent $\frac{5}{8}$ of her monthly salary on expenses. She spent $\frac{1}{4}$ of her remaining salary on a purse, and the rest of her salary was spent on 5 outfits. If each outfit cost $207, what was Sarah's monthly salary?

Unit 5: RATIO

1. Jessica's score is $\frac{2}{7}$ of Kimberly's score in a video game.

    What is the ratio of Kimberly's score to their total scores?

    Jessica : Kimberly

    2 : 7

    Kimberly : Total scores

    7 : 2 + 7

    7 : 9

    The ratio of Kimberly's score to their total scores is **7:9**.

2. During a sale, the price of a pair of shoes is $\frac{1}{4}$ of its original price.

    If its sales price is $97, find the original price of the pair of shoes.

    sales price : original price

    $97 \times \left(\begin{array}{c} 1:4 \\ 97:388 \end{array} \right) \times 97$

    The original price of the pair of shoes is **$388**.

Singapore Math Practice Level 6A

Write your answers on the lines. You may use a calculator whenever you see .

1. The ratio of clothing to bedsheets at a laundromat is 42:54. What fraction of the total pieces of clothing and bedsheets is bedsheets?

    _____

2. Vanida's allowance is $\frac{4}{3}$ of Beatriz's allowance. Find the ratio of Vanida's allowance to their total allowance.

    _____

3. Jon scored 6 times as high as Mandy on a test. Find the ratio of Jon's test score to Mandy's test score to their total test scores.

    _____

4. The ratio of blue ribbons to yellow ribbons is 4:3. If there are 21 yellow ribbons, how many ribbons are there altogether?

    _____

5. The ratio of Melody's age to her father's age is 2:7. The ratio of her mother's age to her father's age is 6:7. Find the ratio of Melody's age to her mother's age.

    _____

6. The ratio of boys to girls in a group is 3:5. If there are 6 boys, how many girls are there?

    _____

7. Boris and Taye shared $550 in the ratio 7:4. Find the amount of money each boy had.

    _____

Singapore Math Practice Level 6A

8. There are 96 carrots in a bag. The carrots are shared among three children in the ratio 4:5:7. Find the smallest share.

_____

9. Grandpa's mass is $\frac{9}{5}$ of Grandma's mass. If their total mass is 112 kg, find Grandpa's mass.

_____

10. To make punch, Diana mixes a can of orange juice concentrate to every 3 cans of lemon-lime soda. How many cans of orange juice concentrate are needed if she uses 36 cans of lemon-lime soda?

_____

11. Sharon used 3 cups of water with every 2 cups of lemon juice to make lemonade. Find the ratio of the amount of lemon juice used to the amount of water used.

_____

12. Mrs. Han used a bag of green beans to make 12 bowls of green bean soup. If she made 84 bowls of green bean soup, how many bags of green beans did she use?

_____

13. The ratio of Sorin's weekly allowance to Joel's weekly allowance was 4:7. After Sorin received $50 from his parents, the ratio became 8:7. How much more money did Joel have than Sorin in the beginning?

_____

14. The ratio of Erick's marbles to Henry's marbles was 3:2. After Erick lost 15 marbles to Henry, the ratio became 2:3. How many marbles did Erick have at first?

_____

Singapore Math Practice Level 6A

15. The ratio of Kelly's money to Vera's money was 7:3. After Kelly spent $35, she had $9 more than Vera. How much money did each girl have at first?

_____

Solve the following story problems. Show your work in the space below.

16. The ratio of men to women to children at a concert was 3:5:2. If there were 360 more adults than children, how many people were at the concert?

Singapore Math Practice Level 6A

17. The ratio of pencils to pens is 3:2. The ratio of pens to rulers is 5:4. If there are 150 pencils and pens altogether, how many rulers are there?

18. Simone's age is $\frac{4}{5}$ of her sister's age.

    (a)   What is the ratio of Simone's age to her sister's age?

    (b)   What fraction of the total age of both girls is her sister's age?

19. The sides of a triangle are in the ratio 3:4:5. If the longest side of the triangle is 40 in. longer than the shortest side, find the perimeter of the triangle.

20. Anita and Winnie share some oranges and lemons in the ratio 5:7. The oranges and lemons that Anita has is in the ratio 3:5. If Anita has 30 fewer oranges than lemons, how many oranges and lemons does Winnie have altogether?

21. The ratio of Lulu's money to Isaac's money is 3:7. The ratio of Isaac's money to Amanda's money is 4:3.

(a) If Lulu has $45 less than Amanda, how much money does Isaac have?

(b) How much money do the three children have altogether?

22. A rectangular metal block measures 30 cm long, 28 cm wide, and 20 cm thick. It is made of copper and zinc in the ratio 7:3 by volume. If 1 cm³ of copper has a mass of 7.6 g and 1 cm³ of zinc has a mass of 6.5 g, find the mass of the metal block. Round your answer to the nearest kg.

Singapore Math Practice Level 6A

23. There were 64 boys and girls at a party. After an hour, 24 boys left and 30 more girls came to the party. The ratio of boys to girls at the party then became 2:5. How many boys were there in the beginning?

24. After Jenny gave Minya 16 stickers, both had the same number of stickers. Lindy then gave 24 stickers to Jenny and the ratio of Jenny's stickers to Minya's original number of stickers became 5:1. How many stickers did Jenny have at first?

25. Arthur and Sam shared some postcards. If Arthur gave 20 postcards to Sam, they would have the same number of postcards. If Sam gave Arthur 10 postcards, the ratio of the number of postcards Arthur had to the number of postcards Sam had would become 2:1. How many postcards did Arthur have in the end?

26. Aaron uses 5 pieces of purple-colored paper and 4 pieces of cream-colored paper to make a brochure.

(a) Find the ratio of the pieces of purple-colored paper to the total pieces of paper Aaron uses for each brochure.

(b) If Aaron has to make 320 brochures for an event, find the total pieces of cream-colored paper he uses.

Singapore Math Practice Level 6A

27. The amount of turkey to ham at the deli in the supermarket was 7:3 in the morning. By the end of the day, 15 lb. of turkey had been sold. The ratio of turkey to ham was now 3:2.

(a) How many pounds of turkey did the deli have in the morning?

(b) How many pounds of ham did the deli have in the morning?

28. The ratio of the number of laps Alfonso swam to the number of laps Basir swam on the first day of a swimming lesson was 5:6. The ratio of the number of laps Alfonso swam to the number of laps Basir swam on the second day of the swimming lesson was 9:5. If Basir swam 33 laps on both days, how many laps did Alfonso swim on the second day of the swimming lesson?

Singapore Math Practice Level 6A

29. The mass of sugar Jolin used to bake a cake was $\frac{3}{5}$ of the mass of flour used. The mass of butter she used was $\frac{5}{6}$ of the mass of sugar used.

(a) Find the ratio of the mass of sugar used to the mass of flour used to the total mass of the three ingredients.

(b) She used 100 g more flour than sugar. How much butter did she use to bake a cake?

30. Dolores cooks 100 g of elbow macaroni with every 300 g of pasta shells for 5 servings of pasta salad.

   (a) What fraction of the amount of pasta shells is the amount of elbow macaroni?

   (b) She needs to cook 35 servings for a family gathering. How much of the pasta shells and elbow macaroni does she need altogether?

Unit 6: PERCENTAGE

Examples:

1. Express $\frac{9}{25}$ as a percentage.

    $\frac{9}{25} \times 100 = \underline{\textbf{36\%}}$

2. Express 63% as a decimal.

    $63\% = \frac{63}{100} = \underline{\textbf{0.63}}$

3. The price of 1 lb. of vegetables was $2.50. Before the Fourth of July, its price was $4.20. Find the percentage increase in price.

    $4.20 - $2.50 = $1.70

    $\frac{\$1.70}{\$2.50} \times 100\% = 68\%$

    The percentage increase in price was **68%**.

4. Tiffany's fee for her dental treatment after sales tax was $133.75.

    (a) How much was her fee for the dental treatment without the 7% sales tax?

    (b) How much did she pay for the 7% sales tax?

    (a)   100% + 7% → $133.75
                1% → $133.75 ÷ 107 = $1.25
            100% → $1.25 × 100 = $125

    Her fee for the dental treatment without the 7% sales tax was **$125**.

    (b) $133.75 − $125 = $8.75

    She paid **$8.75** for the 7% sales tax.

79

Write the following as a percentage. You may use a calculator whenever you see .

1. 4 out of 5   _____

2. 13 out of 100   _____

3. 8 out of 400   _____

 4. 42 out of 250   _____

5. $\dfrac{17}{50}$ _____

6. $\dfrac{1}{20}$ _____

7. $\dfrac{16}{25}$ _____

 8. $\dfrac{96}{800}$ _____

 9. $\dfrac{216}{360}$ _____

 10. $\dfrac{405}{900}$ _____

11. 0.68   _____

12. 0.07   _____

13. 0.215   _____

14. 0.804   _____

15. 0.3   _____

Singapore Math Practice Level 6A

Write each percentage as a fraction in its simplest form.

16. 48% _____

17. 9% _____

18. 15% _____

19. 0.2% _____

20. 98% _____

Write each percentage as a decimal.

21. 73% _____

22. 68% _____

23. 84% _____

24. 3% _____

25. 7% _____

26. The price of 1 lb. of sirloin steak increases from $28 to $35. Find the percentage increase in price.

_____

27. Gina had 3 kg of flour. She used 750 g of flour to bake some cookies. What percentage of the flour did she use?

_____

28. 1,200 people visited a museum. 240 of the visitors were children. What percentage of the visitors were children?

_____

29. Kerry has 300 marbles. 25% of the marbles are green, 15% of the marbles are red, and the rest of the marbles are blue. How many blue marbles does he have?

_____

30. Gary had $230. He spent 45% of the money on a wallet. How much money did he have left?

_____

31. In a class of 40 students, 35% of them walk to school. Half the number of the remaining students take the school bus. How many students take the school bus?

_____

32. There are 600 guests at a party. 48% of them are male adults while 25% of the guests are children. How many female adults are there?

_____

33. The usual price of a shirt was $48. It was sold at a 20% discount. How much was the shirt sold for?

_____

34. After a promotion, Mr. Franco's salary increased by 15%. If he earned $1,600 before, what is his new salary?

_____

35. Amiri dined at a resturant. The total bill came up to $48.15, including the 7% sales tax. How much was the bill before the sales tax?

_____

Singapore Math Practice Level 6A

36. Hazel opened a deposit account with $10,200. The interest was 4% per year. How much interest did Hazel receive after a year?

_____

37. Nari bought a pair of pants for $36 at a sale. If the original price of the pants was $45, what was the percentage discount?

_____

38. Five years ago, Tom had a mass of 56 kg. His mass is 63 kg now. Find the percentage increase in his mass.

_____

39. There are 1,200 students in a school. There are 720 boys, and the rest are girls. What is the difference between the percentage of boys and girls in the school?

_____

40. Jammal bought a diamond ring at a 20% discount. He paid $2,640 for the ring. Naomi bought a similar ring but was given a discount of $924. What was the percentage discount given to Naomi?

_____

Singapore Math Practice Level 6A

Solve the following story problems. Show your work in the space below.

41. Michael bought an MP3 player for $299 and a cordless phone for $148. How much would he pay in total if both items were subjected to a 7% sales tax?

42. Manuel and John have 153 marbles altogether. Manuel has 30% fewer marbles than John. How many marbles does John have?

Singapore Math Practice Level 6A

43. Rebecca gave 30% of her weekly salary to her parents and spent 14% of her weekly salary on food. She also spent $160 on clothes and had $120 left. How much was Rebecca's weekly salary?

44. The number of children enrolled in a summer camp in 2008 was 790. In 2009, the number of children enrolled in the camp increased by 40%. Find the total number of children enrolled in the summer camp in both years.

45. Cheryl bought a leather sofa for $1,609.65 at a warehouse sale. The discount given to her was 65%. What was the original price of the leather sofa?

46. Marisol completed 20% of her worksheets on the first day of vacation. Then, she completed 45% of the worksheets over the next 6 days.

(a) If she completed 18 worksheets each day for 6 days, how many worksheets did she complete on the first day?

(b) How many worksheets did Marisol do altogether?

Singapore Math Practice Level 6A

47. The price of a laptop dropped from $3,099 to $2,135 within 6 months. Find the percentage of decrease in the price. Round your answer to the nearest whole number.

48. A man gave 25% of his money to his wife. He donated $\frac{3}{5}$ of the remaining money to charity and had $4,200 left. How much money did he give to his wife?

Singapore Math Practice Level 6A

49. Jong deposited $5,000 in a savings account. The amount of money in his savings account was $5,075 at the end of the first year. He continued to put that sum of money, including the interest, in the account for a year.

(a) Find the interest rate on the money Jong deposited.

(b) How much money would he get if he decided to close his savings account after the second year? Write your answer to 2 decimal places.

50. Mr. López paid $627.02 for a meal. The cost of the meal included tax.

    (a) If the sales tax on the cost of the meal was 7%, how much did Mr. López pay for the sales tax?

    (b) If the cost of the meal before sales tax was split among 8 people, how much did each person pay?

REVIEW 3

Choose the correct answer, and write its number in the parentheses. You may use a calculator whenever you see 🖩.

1. Write 39% as a decimal.

   (1) 0.39   (3) 30.9

   (2) 3.9   (4) 39   (   )

2. Write $\frac{3}{5}$ as a percentage.

   (1) 6%   (3) 35%

   (2) 30%   (4) 60%   (   )

3. There are 20 children on a playground. 12 of them are boys. Find the ratio of the number of girls to the number of boys at the playground.

   (1) 2:3   (3) 3:2

   (2) 2:5   (4) 5:3   (   )

4. The length and width of a rectangle are in the ratio 5:8. Find the perimeter of the rectangle if its length is 25 in.

   (1) 40 in.   (3) 105 in.

   (2) 65 in.   (4) 130 in.   (   )

5. Mr. Reynolds gave 45% of his monthly salary to his wife. He spent 30% of his salary and saved the rest. If he saved $210 less than what he spent, how much money did he give to his wife?

   (1) $1,050   (3) $1,890

   (2) $1,260   (4) $4,200   (   )

Singapore Math Practice Level 6A

6. The ratio of boy scouts to girl scouts is 8:7. If there are 675 boy and girl scouts in all, find the number of girl scouts.

    (1) 45   (3) 315
    (2) 56   (4) 360   (   )

7. Denise bought a backpack at a 20% discount. She paid $42 for the backpack. How much was the discount?

    (1) $8.40   (3) $33.60
    (2) $10.50   (4) $52.50   (   )

Write your answers on the lines provided.

8. Write 24% as a fraction in its simplest form.   _____

9. Tim and Lisa shared 90 stamps in the ratio 7:3. Tim gave Lisa 5 stamps. Find the new ratio of Tim's stamps to Lisa's stamps.

                                                                          _____

10. Zachary has $360. He spends 42% of the money on a tennis racket. How much does he have left?

                                                                          _____

11. A restaurant bill of $82.50 includes a 10% tip. Find the cost of the meal.

                                                                          _____

12. The ratio of Bobby's age to Eileen's age is 7:6. If Eileen is 18 years old now, how old will Bobby be in 8 years?

                                                                          _____

Singapore Math Practice Level 6A

13. 39% of the books in a library are English books. 25% are Spanish books, 16% are Chinese books, and the rest are French books. If there are 3,000 books in the library, how many French books are there?

_____

14. Jack and Victor were given some raisins in the ratio 8:5. If Jack received 72 raisins, how many more raisins did Jack receive than Victor?

_____

15. Clifford, Zahara, and Marcos shared a sum of money in the ratio 7:5:11. If Zahara received $540, find the sum of money.

_____

Solve the following story problems. Show your work in the space below.

16. Philip has 600 blue and red beads. The ratio of blue beads to red beads is 3:5. If he loses 49 blue beads and 243 red beads, what is the new ratio of blue beads to red beads?

Singapore Math Practice Level 6A

17. Xavier, Yolanda, and Zara shared some money. Yolanda received 40% more money than Xavier, and Zara received 60% of Yolanda's share. If Zara received $1,176, what was the sum of money?

18. Sandra used 15% of the flour to make a pizza and 34% of the flour to bake some cookies. She had 720 g more remaining flour than the amount of flour used to make a pizza. How much flour did Sandra have at first?

Singapore Math Practice Level 6A

19. Corrine's monthly salary is 25% more than Fina's monthly salary. If Fina's salary for 6 months is $27,000, find Corrine's annual salary.

20. The ratio of cars to motorcycles on the road during rush hour is 5:4. The ratio of motorcycles to trucks on the road during rush hour is 8:5.

(a) If the total number of cars and motorcycles on the road during rush hour is 1,044, how many more motorcycles than trucks are there?

(b) How many vehicles are there on the road during rush hour?

FINAL REVIEW

Choose the correct answer, and write its number in the parentheses.

1. What is the value of the digit 4 in 135.847?

    (1) 4 tenths   (3) 4 hundredths

    (2) 4 tens   (4) 4 hundreds   (   )

2. What is the value of 0.87 × 100?

    (1) 0.0087   (3) 87

    (2) 8.7   (4) 870   (   )

3. 4 m 5 cm is the same as _____ cm.

    (1) 405   (3) 4,005

    (2) 450   (4) 4,500   (   )

4. There are 37 students in a martial arts class. There are 9 more male students than female students. What fraction of the students are male?

    (1) $\dfrac{14}{37}$ (3) $\dfrac{28}{37}$

    (2) $\dfrac{23}{37}$ (4) $\dfrac{29}{37}$ (   )

5. Write $2\dfrac{3}{4}$ as a decimal.

    (1) 2.15   (3) 2.43

    (2) 2.34   (4) 2.75   (   )

6. 0.811 m rounded to the nearest centimeter is _____.

    (1) 0.8 cm   (3) 81 cm

    (2) 80 cm   (4) 811 cm   (   )

Singapore Math Practice Level 6A

7. In the figure below, ADB and BDE are right triangles. ABC is a straight line. Find the angle marked h.

   (1) 21°
   (2) 24°
   (3) 42°
   (4) 48°

   ( )

8. The ratio of the length of a rectangle to its width is 6:1. If the length is 36x in., the perimeter of the rectangle is _____ in.

   (1) 42x   (3) 84x
   (2) 48x   (4) 252x   ( )

9. The average of four numbers is 7. If 12 is added to the four numbers, what will the new average be?

   (1) 7   (3) 9
   (2) 8   (4) 10   ( )

10. Roger saved 15% more than Wayne. If Roger saved $2,300, how much did Wayne save?

   (1) $2,000   (3) $4,300
   (2) $4,255   (4) $4,945   ( )

11. Natasha was given a sum of pocket money on Monday. She used $3.80 to buy a book on Tuesday. On Wednesday, Natasha ran some errands for her mother and was given $7. On Thursday, she spent 65¢ on a pencil. If she had $9.50 left, how much pocket money was she given on Monday?

   (1) $5.05   (3) $12.05
   (2) $6.95   (4) $20.95   ( )

12. Cynthia had $8 on her bus pass. Each trip would use up $\frac{4}{5}$ of a dollar. How many trips could she travel using her bus pass?

   (1) 6 trips   (3) 10 trips
   (2) 8 trips   (4) 12 trips   ( )

Singapore Math Practice Level 6A

13. The rates for a hotel room are shown below.

Weekdays	$48 per day
Saturdays and Sundays	$70 per day

Mr. Mizer stayed in the hotel for a week. How much did he pay?

(1) $336   (3) $446

(2) $380   (4) $490   (   )

14. At a shop, a book costs $1.90 more than a pen. A pen costs $3 less than a pencil case. If the total cost of the three items is $13.30, how much does the book cost?

(1) $2.80   (3) $4.90

(2) $4.70   (4) $5.80   (   )

15. Lurene spent 25% of her money on a pair of shoes and the rest on some dresses. If Lurene spent $150 on the dresses, how much was the pair of shoes?

(1) $37.50   (3) $112.50

(2) $50   (4) $450   (   )

Write your answers on the lines.

16. ABC and DEF are identical triangles. What is the sum of $\angle x$, $\angle y$ and $\angle z$?

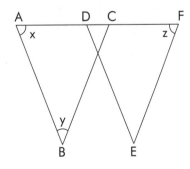

_____

17. Find the value of $2\frac{1}{8} - 1\frac{3}{4}$.   _____

Singapore Math Practice Level 6A

18. Shade the unit shape in the tessellation below.

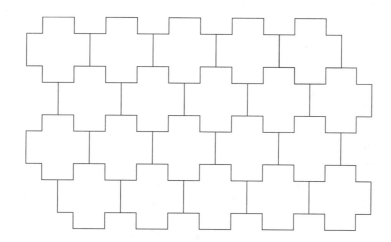

19. Paul bought a digital camera for $300. He sold his camera to a colleague at a discount of 15%. How much did he sell the digital camera for?

_____

20. Natalie bought 4 similar skirts and 6 similar dresses for $426. If one skirt and one dress cost $96, find the cost of each dress.

_____

21. Draw a line of symmetry for the figure below.

Singapore Math Practice Level 6A

The graph below shows the distance traveled by a van and the amount of gasoline it had left. Study the graph below and answer questions 22 to 24.

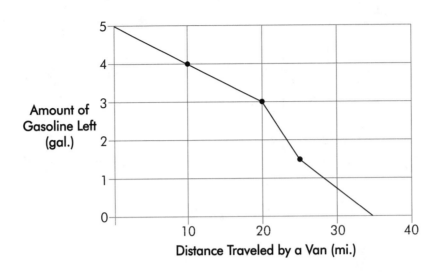

22. How much gasoline was consumed after the van had traveled 20 miles?

23. How far did the van travel with 5 gal. of gasoline?

24. On the average, how far did the van travel with 1 gal. of gasoline?

25. Measure ∠z.

26. Find the value of $\dfrac{6y + 4y + 5}{11}$ when $y = 5$.

Singapore Math Practice Level 6A

27. Spencer called Jacob at quarter past two in the afternoon and promised to meet Jacob in half an hour. However, Spencer was 15 minutes late. At what time did Spencer arrive?

_____

28. 2 hundredths 8 tenths 28 ones written as a decimal is [   ].

_____

29. If A is 4 times B and B is 6 times C, find the ratio A:B:C.

_____

30. The figure below shows two triangles in a rectangle. Find the area of the unshaded part.

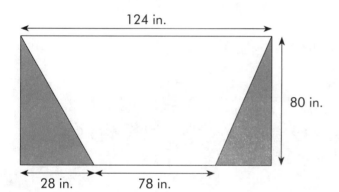

124 in.

80 in.

28 in.   78 in.

_____

Write your answers on the lines. You may use a calculator.

31. $\frac{1}{8} + \frac{3}{8} = \boxed{} \times \frac{1}{4}$

_____

32. Find the value of $\angle a$.

_____

33. What is 20% of 3 m 25 cm?

_____

34. Adam bought 3 books at $9.25 each. How much change would he receive if he gave the cashier a fifty-dollar bill?

_____

35. A can of sardines has a mass of 325 g. 60 cans of sardines are packed for delivery in a box. If the empty box has a mass of 1.44 kg, what is the total mass of a box of 60 tins of sardines? Write your answer to the nearest kilogram.

_____

Solve the following story problems. Show your work in the space below. You may use a calculator.

36. There are 45 waitresses and 50 waiters in a chain of restaurants. 60% of them are new staff, 50% of the remaining staff are temporary, and the rest are permanent staff. How many permanent staff are there?

Singapore Math Practice Level 6A

37. The table below shows the fare for hiring a taxi. How much would Rieko have to pay if she traveled 7.8 miles?

First mile	$2.50
Every $\frac{1}{4}$ mi. thereafter or less for the next 5 mi.	$0.40
Every $\frac{1}{10}$ mi. thereafter or less after 6 mi.	$0.20

Singapore Math Practice Level 6A

38. A shopkeeper bought 8 boxes of apples. There were 15y apples in each box. He sold 8y apples and threw away 17 rotten apples.

(a)   How many apples did he have left? Write your answer in terms of y.

(b)   If y = 20, how many apples did he have left?

39. Lenny had 86 marbles and Bob had 22 marbles. After each of them received the same number of marbles from Emilio, Lenny had twice as many marbles as Bob. How many marbles did Emilio give to both of them?

40. $90 is shared between Claire, Eliza, and Vicky. Claire receives $\frac{5}{8}$ of the money and Eliza receives $\frac{2}{3}$ of the remainder. How much more does Claire receive than Vicky?

41. At a city-wide assembly, 28% of the participants were fourth graders. There were 7% more fifth graders than fourth graders. If the number of sixth graders was 910 fewer than the total number of fifth graders and fourth graders, how many sixth graders attended the assembly?

42. The average mass of Harry and William is 65.2 kg. The average mass of William and Charlie is 58.6 kg.

(a)   Find the average mass of Harry and Charlie if William has a mass of 62.3 kg.

(b)   Find the total mass of the three boys.

43. The ratio of the perimeter of a square field to that of a rectangular field is 3:2. If each side of the square field is 9 yd., find

   (a)   the perimeter of the rectangular field.

   (b)   the width of the rectangular field if its length is 8 yd.

44. $\frac{3}{5}$ of Donna's coins were nickels, 25% of them were quarters, and the rest were dimes. If there were $20 worth of quarters, find the total amount of money that Donna had.

45. Mr. Anderson pays $375 for his cell phone every month. Mrs. Anderson pays $\frac{2}{5}$ as much as Mr. Anderson for her cell phone every month. They decided to cut down on their cell phone bills. Mr. Anderson's bill is reduced by $\frac{1}{5}$ in the following month and Mrs. Anderson bill is reduced by $\frac{1}{6}$.

(a)   How much does Mrs. Anderson pay for her cell phone bill every month?

(b)   How much do both of them pay for their cell phone bills in the following month?

46. There are 600 people at a beach. $\frac{2}{3}$ of them are men, while the rest are women and children. $\frac{1}{3}$ of the number of women equals $\frac{1}{2}$ of the number of children. If $\frac{1}{10}$ of the women and $\frac{1}{4}$ of the children cannot swim, how many women and children can swim?

47. A jar of cookies is 630 g when it is $\frac{1}{2}$ full and 855 g when it is $\frac{7}{9}$ full.

   (a)   How many kilograms of cookies can the jar hold when it is full?

   (b)   What is the mass of the empty jar?

48. Marie bought some albums and picture frames as gifts for a party. Each album cost $18 and each picture frame cost $3 less. The ratio of picture frames to albums was 4:3. She paid a total of $1,026 for all the albums and picture frames.

(a) How many albums and picture frames did she buy in all?

(b) If Marie did not buy any picture frames, how many more albums could she buy with the same amount of money?

CHALLENGE QUESTIONS

Solve the following problems on another sheet of paper.

1. There were 244 pencils altogether. Sean put them into 3 different boxes. There were 70% more pencils in box A than in box B. There were twice as many pencils in Box C than in Box A. How many pencils were in each box?

2. 133 yen equals $0.75 Euros
   $1 equals 99 Japanese yen

   Giancarla, a sixth-grade celloist from Europe, went on tour with her orchestra. She arrived in the United States with $1,000, and she spent $890. Then the orchestra had two days in Japan, where she spent 10,000 yen. When she got home, she exchanged the remaining Japanese yen for Euros. How much money did she have in Euros? Round your answer to the nearest Euro.

3. Use only two addition signs (+) and four subtraction signs (–) to make the number sentence correct.

   $$90 \ \_\_\_ \ 80 \ \_\_\_ \ 70 \ \_\_\_ \ 60 \ \_\_\_ \ 50 \ \_\_\_ \ 40 \ \_\_\_ \ 30 = 20$$

4. On a school quiz, a team had to answer 25 questions. The team was given 50 points at the beginning of the school quiz. If the team answered a question correctly, it would be given 2 points. If the team gave a wrong answer, 1 point would be deducted. At the end of the school quiz, the team had 76 points. How many questions did it get wrong?

5. Fill in each box with numbers from 1 to 16.

   Each row should add up to 34.

				34
				34
				34
				34

Singapore Math Practice Level 6A

6. X and Y are numbers between 50 and 100. Both X and Y have the same digits but in a different order. The two numbers add to 187. All their digits add up to 34. Find X and Y.

7. $1 equals 99 yen
   13.79 pesos equal $1

   Ben Ochoa is a foreign baseball player in Japan. He sends money home to his family. He exchanged 500,000 Japanese yen into dollars. He sent half of the money home in pesos. How many pesos did he send home? Round your answer to the nearest peso.

8. Agnes flipped through a 100-page book. She stopped flipping on a page. The product of the page numbers facing each other was 4,032. What were the page numbers?

9. Ray got his first pay increment in 2005. Since then, he has received a 15% increment every year. If his monthly pay in 2008 was $5,290, what was his monthly pay in 2006?

10. 30 businessmen attended a conference. If each businessman shook hands with everyone once, how many handshakes were exchanged?

11. Complete the number pattern below.

    23, 46, 92, 184, 368, _____, _____, _____

12. Fill in each box with numbers from 1 to 9.

    The product of the three numbers in a row should be the 10th, 12th, and 14th multiples of 6.

			12th multiple of 6
			14th multiple of 6
			10th multiple of 6

SOLUTIONS
Singapore Math Practice Level 6A

Unit 1: Algebra

1. $\frac{x}{40}$ **pencils**
   $x \div 40 = \frac{x}{40}$

2. **$10y**
   $10 \times \$y = \$10y$

3. **(m + 2) years old**

4. **(z − 5) apples**

5. $\left(44 + \frac{x}{2}\right)$ **points**
   $\frac{88 + x}{2} = \left(44 + \frac{x}{2}\right)$

6. **6n stamps**
   Ahmed: $2 \times n = 2n$
   Peter: $3 \times 2n = 6n$

7. **$(25 + a)**
   Amount of money Mey gave to her sister = $50 ÷ 2
                                           = \$25
   Amount of money Mey had left = \$50 − \$25
                                = \$25
   $\$25 + a = \$(25 + a)$

8. **(x + y + z) balloons**

9. **(z − 17) cakes**
   $5 + 12 = 17$
   $z − 17$

10. **50 − 3x gallons of gasoline**
    $x + 2x = 3x$
    $50 − 3x = (50 − 3x)$

11. **16**
    $1 + 6 + 9 = 16$

12. **5**
    $6 − 3 + 2 = 5$

13. **18**
    $6 + 6 + 6 = 18$

14. **12**
    $2 \times 6 = 12$

15. **36**
    $6 \times 6 = 36$

16. **3**
    $6 \div 2 = 3$

17. **30**
    $(3 \times 6) + (2 \times 6) = 18 + 12 = 30$

18. **4**
    $(8 \times 6) \div 12 = 48 \div 12 = 4$

19. **39**
    $(3 \times 6) + (4 \times 6) − 3 = 18 + 24 − 3 = 39$

20. **44**
    $(10 \times 6) − (4 \times 6) + 21 − 13 = 60 − 24 + 21 − 13 = 44$

21. **4a**
    $a + a + 2a = 4a$

22. **8b**
    $5b − 3b + 6b = 2b + 6b = 8b$

23. **c**
    $3c + 2c − 4c = 5c − 4c = c$

24. **3d**
    $6d − d − 2d = 5d − 2d = 3d$

25. **9 + 2e**
    $4 + 5 + 2e = 9 + 2e$

26. **14 + 5f**
    $9 + 5 + f + 4f = 14 + 5f$

27. **2g − 3**
    $4g − 2g − 3 = 2g − 3$

28. **h + 4**
    $7h − 5h − h + 4 = h + 4$

29. **2x − 6**
    $3x − x − 6 = 2x − 6$

30. **13 + 24k**
    $10 + 3 + 10k + 14k = 13 + 24k$

31. **3a**
    $18a \div 6 = 3a$

32. **$(50 − 20m)**
    $10 \times \$2m = \$20m$
    $\$50 − \$20m = \$(50 − 20m)$

33. **92 cm**
    $3b + 10 + 3b + 10 = (3 \times 12) + 10 + (3 \times 12) + 10$
    $\qquad\qquad\qquad\quad = 36 + 10 + 36 + 10$
    $\qquad\qquad\qquad\quad = 92$

34. **196 in.²**
    $7 \times 2 = 14$ cm
    $14 \times 14 = 196$ in.²

35. **57**
    $a + 3b \times 2 − b = 7 + (3 \times 10) \times 2 − 10$
    $\qquad\qquad\qquad = 57$

36. **16**
    $14a = 84$
    $\quad a = 84 \div 14 = 6$
    $6 + 10 = 16$

37. **6**
    $(4 \times 3) − (2 \times 3) = 12 − 6 = 6$

38. **28**
    $\frac{1}{2} \times n = 14$
    $\qquad n = 14 \times 2 = 28$

39. **15k**
    $9 \times 2k = 18k$
    $18k − 3k = 15k$

40. **$(y + 6)**
    Shoes: $2 \times \$3y = \$6y$
    $\$3y + \$6y = \$9y$
    $\$(10y + 6) − \$9y = \$10y − \$9y + \$6$
    $\qquad\qquad\qquad = \$(y + \$6)$

115

Singapore Math Practice Level 6A

41. From 2:30 P.M. to 3:30 P.M. = $2
From 3:30 P.M. to 4:30 P.M. = $d
From 4:30 P.M. to 5:10 P.M. = $d
$2 + $d + $d = $(2 + 2d)
He had to pay $**(2 + 2d)** for parking.

42. (a) $x \div 2 = \dfrac{x}{2}$

    Judi must give $\dfrac{x}{2}$ pieces of candy to Wendy so that both will have an equal number of pieces of candy.
    (b) $80 - x = 80 - 40 = 40$
    Wendy has 40 pieces of candy.
    $80 + 40 = 120$
    They have **120** pieces of candy altogether.

43. (a) 6 parts → 18y
    1 part → 18y ÷ 6 = 3y
    5 parts → 5 × 3y = 15y
    The number of marbles Joyce received was **15y**.
    (b) 6 + 5 + 3 = 14
    14 × 3y = 42y
    The total number of marbles the three children had was **42y**.

44. (a) $10 - y = (10 - y)$ cm
    The increase in the water level was **(10 – y) cm**.
    (b) Increase in volume of water
    = Length × Width × Height of increase
    = 18 × 12 × (10 – 8)
    = 432 cm³
    The increase in volume of water after the marbles were placed into the tank was **432 cm³**.

45. (a) $b + $125 = $(b + 125)
    Miss Kazuo had $**(b + 125)**.
    (b) $b + $125 = $75 + $125 = $200
    Miss Kazuo had $**200** in the beginning.

46. (a) 3 × $r = $3r
    A chicken sandwich costs $3r.
    $r + $3r = $4r
    The total cost of a milk shake and a chicken sandwich is $**4r**.
    (b) $3r = 3 × 2 = $6
    A chicken sandwich costs $6.
    (3 × $6) + (2 × $3) = $18 + $6 = $24
    3 chicken sandwiches and 2 large orders of French fries cost $**24**.

47. (a) $y \div 6 = $\left(\dfrac{y}{6}\right)$

    The cost of each fork was $\left(\dfrac{y}{6}\right)$.
    (b) 5 × $y = 5 × $18 = $90
    Olivia paid $**90** for 5 boxes of forks.

48. (a) $x + \dfrac{x}{2} + 3x + 40 = 4x + \dfrac{x}{2} + 40$

    $\left(4x + \dfrac{x}{2} + 40\right)$ people were at the library altogether.
    (b) $(4 × 56) + \dfrac{56}{2} + 40 = 292$
    The total number of people at the library was **292**.

Unit 2: Angles

1. **100°**
   ∠BAC = ∠BCA = 40°   (isosceles Δ)
   ∠ABC = 180° – 40° – 40° = 100°   (sum of ∠s in a Δ = 180°)

2. **95°**
   ∠DOB = 180° – 85° = 95°   (∠s on a striaight line)

3. **75°**
   ∠COD = 180° – 63° – 42° = 75°   (∠s on a straight line)

4. **114°**
   ∠CBA = 180° – 65° – 49° = 66° (sum of ∠s in a Δ = 180°)
   ∠CBD = 180° – 66° = 114°   (∠s on a straight line)

5. **37°**
   ∠PQR = 180° – 74° = 106°   (∠s on a straight line)
   ∠PRQ = $\dfrac{180° - 106°}{2}$ = 37°   (isosceles Δ)

6. **63°**
   ∠WZY = 180° – 117° = 63°
               (∠s between two parallel lines = 180°)

7. **112°**
   ∠ABC = 180° – 68° = 112°   (∠s on a straight line)
   ∠ADC = ∠ABC = 112°   (opposite ∠s are equal)

8. **68°**
   ∠SRQ = ∠QPS = 68°   (opposite ∠s are equal)

9. **73°**
   ∠ACB = 180° – 33° – 74° = 73° (sum of ∠s in a Δ = 180°)
   ∠DCE = ∠ACB = 73°   (vertically opposite ∠s)

10. **120°**
    ∠XYZ = ∠YZX = ∠ZXY = 60°   (equilateral Δ)
    ∠YZW = 180° – 60° = 120°   (∠s on a straight line)

11. **30°**
    ∠ABC = 180° – 108° – 42° = 30° (sum of ∠s in a Δ = 180°)

12. **53°**
    ∠DCE = ∠DEC = $\dfrac{180° - 74°}{2}$ = 53°   (isosceles Δ)
    ∠DCB = 180° – 53° = 127°   (∠s on a straight line)
    ∠ADC = 180° – 127° = 53°
               (∠s between two parallel lines = 180°)

13. **110°**
    ∠SRT = 180° – 90° – 55° = 35°   (sum of ∠s in a Δ = 180°)
    ∠SRQ = 180° – 105° = 75°
               (∠s between two parallel lines = 180°)
    ∠QRT = 35° + 75° = 110°

14. **74°**
    ∠BAC = ∠ABC = ∠BCA = 60°   (equilateral Δ)
    ∠DAE = 60° – 44° = 16°
    ∠EDA = 180° – 16° – 90° = 74° (sum of ∠s in a Δ = 180°)

15. **56°**
    ∠WXY = 180° – 71° = 109°
               (∠s between two parallel lines = 180°)
    ∠YXZ = 109° – 53° = 56°

16. **15°**
    ∠BCX = 180° – 75° = 105°
               (∠s between two parallel lines = 180°)
    ∠ACB = 180° – 105° = 75°   (∠s on a straight line)
    ∠ABC = 180° – 75° – 90° = 15° (sum of ∠s in a Δ = 180°)

Singapore Math Practice Level 6A

17. **107°**
$\angle DCF = 180° - 73° = 107°$ (∠s on a straight line)
$\angle DEF = 107°$ (opposite ∠s are equal)

18. **50°**
$\angle ADC = 180° - 80° = 100°$ (∠s on a straight line)
$\angle BCD = 180° - 100° = 80°$
(∠s between two parallel lines = 180°)
$\angle ADB = \dfrac{180° - 80°}{2} = 50°$ (isosceles Δ)

19. **48°**
$\angle ADC = 63°$ (opposite ∠s are equal)
$\angle BCD = 180° - 63° = 117°$
(∠s between two parallel lines =180°)
$\angle DCE = 180° - 117° = 63°$ (∠s on a straight line)
$\angle CDE = 180° - 63° - 48° = 69°$ (sum of ∠s in a Δ = 180°)
$\angle FDE = 180° - 63° - 69° = 48°$ (∠s on a straight line)

20. **11°**
$\angle ECF = 79°$ (opposite ∠s are equal)
$\angle FCD = 90° - 79° = 11°$

Review 1

1. **(3)**
$16a - 6a = 10a$
$= 10 \times 3 = 30$

2. **(2)**
$6a + 6 + 27a - 3 = 6a + 27a + 6 - 3$
$= 33a + 3$

3. **(1)**
$\angle ACB = 60°$ (equilateral Δ)
$\angle BCD = 180° - 60° = 120°$ (∠s on a straight line)
$\angle CBE = 180° - 120° = 60°$
(∠s between two parallel lines = 180°)

4. **(2)**
$\angle PSR = 75°$ (opposite ∠s are equal)
$\angle PST = 75° - 44° = 31°$
$\angle SPT = 180° - 75° = 105°$
(∠s between two parallel lines = 180°)
$\angle PTS = 180° - 31° - 105° = 44°$ (sum of ∠s in a Δ = 180°)

5. **(3)**
$(4 \times x) + 7 = 4x + 7$

6. **(1)**
$\angle WUX = 180° - 90° - 39° = 51°$ (sum of ∠s in a Δ = 180°)
$\angle XUY = 90° - 51° = 39°$

7. **(3)**
$\$81 - \$23 = \$58$
$\$58 + \$16 = \$74$

8. **12a + 6**
$5a + 9 + 7a - 3 = 5a + 7a + 9 - 3$
$= 12a + 6$

9. **(6b + 20) years old**
$(6 \times b) + 20 = 6b + 20$

10. **122°**
$\angle DEB = 180° - 58° = 122°$ (∠s on a straight line)
$\angle DAB = 122°$ (opposite ∠s are equal)

11. **96**

12. **39°**
$\angle WYX = 180° - 129° = 51°$ (∠s on a straight line)
$\angle WXY = 180° - 90° - 51° = 39°$ (sum of ∠s in a Δ = 180°)

$8y - 29 + 3y - 18 = (8 \times 13) - 29 + (3 \times 13) - 18$
$= 104 - 29 + 39 - 18$
$= 96$

13. **137°**
$\angle ACB = \angle ABC = 54°$ (isosceles Δ)
$\angle CAB = 180° - 54° - 54° = 72°$ (sum of ∠s in a Δ = 180°)
$\angle CDA = 180° - 132° = 48°$ (∠s on a straight line)
$\angle CAD = 180° - 48° - 67° = 65°$ (sum of ∠s in a Δ = 180°)
$\angle DAB = 65° + 72° = 137°$

14. **6v kg**
$3 \times 6v = 18v$
$2 \times 6v = 12v$
$18v + 12v = 30v$
$30v \div 5 = 6v$

15. **$\$\left(\dfrac{m}{12}\right)$**
$\$m \div 12 = \$\left(\dfrac{m}{12}\right)$

16. (a) $(n + 4) + 6 = n + 10$
Their total age is $(n + 10)$ years now.
$(n + 10) + 10 + 10 = n + 30$
Their total age in 10 years is **(n + 30) years.**
(b) $n + 30 = 8 + 30 = 38$
Their total age in 10 years is **38 years.**

17. $\angle BCE = 180° - 63° = 117°$
(∠s between two parallel lines = 180°)
$\angle BCD = 117° - 41° = \mathbf{76°}$

18. $\angle ACB = 60°$ (equilateral Δ)
$\angle BCD = 180° - 30° - 30° = 120°$ (sum of ∠s in a Δ = 180°)
$\angle ECA = 180° - 60° = 120°$ (∠s on a straight line)
$\angle x = 60° + 120° + 120° = \mathbf{300°}$

19. (a) $3 \times m = 3m$
Sachiko has $3m$ cards.
$m + 22 = (m + 22)$
Ivy has $(m + 22)$ cards.
$3m + m + 12 = 4m + 12$
Casey has $(4m + 12)$ cards.
$m + 3m + (m + 22) + (4m + 12) = 9m + 34$
They have **(9m + 34)** cards altogether.
(b) $(9m + 34) \div 4 = \dfrac{9m + 34}{4}$
Each girl gets $\left(\dfrac{\mathbf{9m + 34}}{\mathbf{4}}\right)$ cards.

20. (a) $5 \times \$29 = \$145$
The purse cost $\$145$.
$\$29 + \$145 + \$y = \$(174 + y)$
Alicia had **$(174 + y)** in the beginning.
(b) $\$(174 + y) = \$(174 + 52) = \$226$
Alicia had **$226** in the beginning.

Unit 3: Identifying Solids and Nets

1. **cone**
2. **pyramid**
3. **cuboid**
4. **prism**

117

Singapore Math Practice Level 6A

5. cylinder
6. cube
7. **4, triangle**
8. **6, rectangle**
9. **5, rectangle** and **triangle**
10. **5, triangle** and **rectangle**
11. **6, square** and **trapezium**
12. **6, square**
13. **Yes**
14. **Yes**
15. **Yes**
16. **Yes**
17. **No**
18. **No**
19.

20.

21.

22.

23.

Unit 4: Fractions

1. $\dfrac{9}{14}$

$$\frac{1}{7} + \frac{1}{2} = \frac{2}{14} + \frac{7}{14} = \frac{9}{14}$$

2. **1**

$$\frac{\cancel{12}^{\,3}}{\cancel{8}_{\,3}} \times \frac{\cancel{8}^{\,1}}{\cancel{4}_{\,1}} = \frac{3}{3} = 1$$

3. $\dfrac{3}{10}$

$$\frac{2}{5} - \frac{1}{10} = \frac{4}{10} - \frac{1}{10} = \frac{3}{10}$$

4. $\dfrac{1}{22}$

$$\frac{3}{11} \div 6 = \frac{\cancel{3}^{\,1}}{11} \times \frac{1}{\cancel{6}_{\,2}} = \frac{1}{22}$$

5. $18\dfrac{2}{3}$

$$2\frac{1}{3} \times 8 = \frac{7}{3} \times \frac{8}{1} = \frac{56}{3} = 18\frac{2}{3}$$

6. $4\dfrac{8}{15}$

$$7\frac{1}{5} - 2\frac{2}{3} = \frac{36}{5} - \frac{8}{3} = \frac{108}{15} - \frac{40}{15} = \frac{68}{15} = 4\frac{8}{15}$$

7. $25\dfrac{25}{72}$

$$10\frac{2}{9} + 15\frac{1}{8} = \frac{92}{9} + \frac{121}{8} = \frac{736}{72} + \frac{1,089}{72} = \frac{1,825}{72} = 25\frac{25}{72}$$

8. $1\dfrac{11}{15}$

$$5\frac{1}{5} \div 3 = \frac{26}{5} \div 3 = \frac{26}{5} \times \frac{1}{3} = \frac{26}{15} = 1\frac{11}{15}$$

9. **18**

$$6 \div \frac{1}{3} = \frac{6}{1} \times \frac{3}{1} = 18$$

10. **15**

$$9 \div \frac{3}{5} = \frac{\cancel{9}^{\,3}}{1} \times \frac{5}{\cancel{3}_{\,1}} = 15$$

11. $\dfrac{2}{7}$

$$\frac{1}{7} \div \frac{1}{2} = \frac{1}{7} \times \frac{2}{1} = \frac{2}{7}$$

12. $\dfrac{11}{18}$

$$\frac{4}{9} \div \frac{8}{11} = \frac{\cancel{4}^{\,1}}{9} \times \frac{11}{\cancel{8}_{\,2}} = \frac{11}{18}$$

13. **3**

$$\frac{6}{7} \div \frac{2}{7} = \frac{\cancel{6}^{\,3}}{\cancel{7}_{\,1}} \times \frac{\cancel{7}^{\,1}}{\cancel{2}_{\,1}} = 3$$

14. $40\dfrac{1}{2}$

$$36 \div \frac{8}{9} = \frac{36}{1} \times \frac{9}{8} = \frac{324}{8} = 40\frac{1}{2}$$

15. $\dfrac{1}{2}$

$$\frac{3}{8} \div \frac{3}{4} = \frac{\cancel{3}^{\,1}}{\cancel{8}_{\,2}} \times \frac{\cancel{4}^{\,1}}{\cancel{3}_{\,1}} = \frac{1}{2}$$

16. $\dfrac{21}{40}$ **gal.**

$$\frac{2}{5} + \frac{1}{8} = \frac{16}{40} + \frac{5}{40} = \frac{21}{40}$$

17. **28 volunteers**

$$7 \div \frac{1}{4} = 7 \times \frac{4}{1} = 7 \times 4 = 28$$

18. **7 cakes**

$$\frac{7}{8} \div \frac{1}{8} = \frac{7}{\cancel{8}_{\,1}} \times \frac{\cancel{8}^{\,1}}{1} = 7$$

19. $\dfrac{7}{15}$

$$\frac{1}{3} + \frac{1}{5} = \frac{5}{15} + \frac{3}{15} = \frac{8}{15}$$

$$1 - \frac{8}{15} = \frac{7}{15}$$

20. **7 people**

$$3 \div \frac{3}{7} = \cancel{3}^{\,1} \times \frac{7}{\cancel{3}_{\,1}} = 7$$

21. $$24 \div \frac{3}{4} = \cancel{24}^{\,8} \times \frac{4}{\cancel{3}_{\,1}}$$
$$= 8 \times 4$$
$$= 32$$

She taught **32** lessons in the month of June.

22. $69 + 23 = 92$

$$1 - \frac{3}{5} = \frac{2}{5}$$

$$92 \div \frac{2}{5} = 230$$

Fala made **230** brownies.

23. (a) $\quad 1 - \dfrac{1}{5} - \dfrac{1}{2} = \dfrac{3}{10}$

$$\frac{3}{10} \div \frac{1}{10} = 3$$

Singapore Math Practice Level 6A

Aunt Mary has **3** pets.

(b) $\dfrac{3}{10} \rightarrow \$375$

$\dfrac{1}{10} \rightarrow \$375 \div 3 = \$125$

$10 \times \$125 = \$1,250$

Her household expenses is **\$1,250.**

24. (a) $1 - \dfrac{3}{4} = \dfrac{1}{4}$

$\dfrac{1}{4} \div \dfrac{1}{8} = 2$

Mr. Lee had **2 sons.**

$\dfrac{3}{4} \div \dfrac{1}{4} = 3$

Mr. Lee had **3 daughters.**

(b) $2 \times 3 = 6$

He bought 6 chocolate bars.

$3 \times 6 = 18$

He bought 18 yogurt bars.

$6 + 18 = 24$

Mr. Lee bought **24** snacks.

25. (a) $\dfrac{1}{4} \times 92 = 23$

23 teachers took part in the recycling exercise.

(b) $92 - 23 = 69$

69 students took part in the recycling exercise.
Assume each student brought 1 empty soda can
and each teacher brought 5 empty soda cans.

$69 \times 1 = 69$

$23 \times 5 = 115$

$115 - 69 = 46$

There would be a difference of 46 empty soda cans.

$138 \div 46 = 3$

$1 \times 3 = 3$

Each student brought **3** empty soda cans.

(c) $5 \times 3 = 15$

Each teacher brought 15 empty soda cans.

$(23 \times 15) + (69 \times 3) = 345 + 207 = 552$

552 empty soda cans were collected altogether.

Review 2

1. **(4)**

2. **(2)**

$\dfrac{1}{7} \times \dfrac{8}{9} = \dfrac{8}{63}$

3. **(1)**

$\dfrac{1}{3} + \dfrac{1}{2} = \dfrac{2}{6} + \dfrac{3}{6} = \dfrac{5}{6}$

$1 - \dfrac{5}{6} = \dfrac{1}{6}$

4. **(4)**

5. **(4)**

$\dfrac{3}{5} \div \dfrac{1}{10} = \dfrac{3}{\cancel{5}_1} \times \dfrac{\cancel{10}^2}{1} = 6$

6. **(3)**

$6 \div \dfrac{1}{2} = 6 \times \dfrac{2}{1} = 12$

7. **(2)**

$3 - \dfrac{1}{2} = 2\dfrac{1}{2}$ lb.

$2\dfrac{1}{2} \div 3 = \dfrac{5}{2} \div 3 = \dfrac{5}{2} \times \dfrac{1}{3} = \dfrac{5}{6}$ lb.

8. **pyramid**

9. **21**

$9 \div \dfrac{3}{7} = \dfrac{\cancel{9}^3}{1} \times \dfrac{7}{\cancel{3}_1} = 21$

10. $\dfrac{1}{8}$ **L**

$\dfrac{3}{4} \div 6 = \dfrac{3}{4}^1 \times \dfrac{1}{\cancel{6}_2} = \dfrac{1}{8}$

11. **rectangle** and **triangle**

12. **prism**

13. **152 pages**

$1 - \dfrac{1}{4} - \dfrac{1}{8} = 1 - \dfrac{2}{8} - \dfrac{1}{8} = \dfrac{5}{8}$

$\dfrac{5}{8} \rightarrow 95$ pages

$\dfrac{1}{8} \rightarrow 95 \div 5 = 19$ pages

$8 \times 19 = 152$ pages

14. **32 apples**

$4 \div \dfrac{1}{8} = 4 \times \dfrac{8}{1} = 32$

15. $7\dfrac{11}{12}$ **yd.**

$\dfrac{5}{\cancel{8}_2} \times \cancel{12}^3 = \dfrac{15}{2} = 7\dfrac{1}{2}$ yd.

$7\dfrac{1}{2} + \dfrac{5}{12} = 7\dfrac{6}{12} + \dfrac{5}{12} = 7\dfrac{11}{12}$ yd.

16. (a) This solid has **6** faces when its net is folded.

(b) The shape of the faces is **rectangle.**

17. $1 - \dfrac{2}{5} - \dfrac{3}{10} = 1 - \dfrac{4}{10} - \dfrac{3}{10} = \dfrac{3}{10}$

$\dfrac{3}{10}$ of the audience were professionals.

$\dfrac{2}{5} - \dfrac{3}{10} = \dfrac{4}{10} - \dfrac{3}{10} = \dfrac{1}{10}$

$\dfrac{1}{10} \rightarrow 18$

$10 \times 18 = 180$

180 people were at the seminar.

18. (a) $\dfrac{3}{8} \times 240 = 90$

$90 \div 3 = 30$

Each girl had **30** marbles.

(b) $1 - \dfrac{3}{8} = \dfrac{5}{8}$

$\dfrac{5}{8} \times 240 = 150$

$150 \div 25 = 6$

There were **6** boys.

19.

The figure is a **cube.**

20. $5 \times \$207 = \$1,035$

$1 - \dfrac{5}{8} = \dfrac{3}{8}$

$\dfrac{1}{4} \times \dfrac{3}{8} = \dfrac{3}{32}$

She spent $\dfrac{3}{32}$ of her monthly salary on the purse.

$1 - \dfrac{5}{8} - \dfrac{3}{32} = \dfrac{9}{32}$

She spent $\dfrac{9}{32}$ of her monthly salary on the outfits.

$\dfrac{9}{32} \rightarrow \$1,035$

$\dfrac{1}{32} \rightarrow \$1,035 \div 9 = \$115$

$32 \times \$115 = \$3,680$

Sarah's monthly salary was **$3,680**.

Unit 5: Ratio

1. $\dfrac{9}{16}$

   $\dfrac{54}{42 + 54} = \dfrac{54}{96} = \dfrac{9}{16}$

2. **4:7**

   $\dfrac{\text{Vanida}}{\text{Beatriz}} = \dfrac{4}{3}$

   Vanida:Total allowance
       4:3 + 4
       4:7

3. **6:1:7**

   Jon:Mandy:Total score
       6:1:6 + 1
       6:1:7

4. **49 ribbons**

   3 units → 21 yellow ribbons
   1 unit → 21 ÷ 3 = 7 ribbons
   7 units → 7 × 7 = 49 ribbons

5. **2:6**

   Melody:Father:Mother
       2:7:6
   Melody:Mother
       2:6

6. **10 girls**

   boys:girls
       3:5
   3 units → 6 boys
   1 unit → 6 ÷ 3 = 2
   5 units → 5 × 2 = 10 girls

7. **Boris: $350**
   Taye: $200
   7 + 4 units → $550
       11 units → $550
           1 unit → $550 ÷ 11 = $50
           7 units → 7 × $50 = $350
           4 units → 4 × $50 = $200

8. **24 carrots**
   4 + 5 + 7 units → 96 carrots
           16 units → 96 carrots

1 unit → 96 ÷ 16 = 6 carrots
4 units → 4 × 6 = 24 carrots

9. **72 kg**
   Grandpa:Grandma
       9:5
   9 + 5 units → 112 kg
       14 units → 112 kg
           1 unit → 112 ÷ 14 = 8 kg
           9 units → 9 × 8 = 72 kg

10. **12 cans of orange juice concentrate**

    $\dfrac{\text{orange juice}}{\text{lemon-lime soda}} = \dfrac{1}{3} = \dfrac{12}{36}$

11. **2:3**
    lemon juice:water
        2:3

12. **7 bags of green beans**
    12 bowls of green bean soup → 1 bag
    84 bowls of green bean soup → 84 ÷ 12 = 7 bags

13. **$37.50**
    8 − 4 units → $50
        4 units → $50
        1 unit → $50 ÷ 4 = $12.50
    7 − 4 = 3 units
    3 × $12.50 = $37.50

14. **45 marbles**

    ```
              ?
    Erick  [    | 15 ]
    Henry  [    | 15 ]
    ```

    1 unit → 15
    3 units → 3 × 15 = 45

15. **Kelly: $77**
    Vera: $33
    7 − 3 = 4 units
    4 units → $35 + $9 = $44
    1 unit → $44 ÷ 4 = $11
    7 units → 7 × $11 = $77
    3 units → 3 × $11 = $33

16. $\dfrac{\text{Number of adults}}{\text{number of children}} = \dfrac{3 + 5}{2} = \dfrac{8}{2}$

    8 − 2 units → 360
        6 units → 360
        1 unit → 360 ÷ 6 = 60
    8 + 2 units → 10 × 60 = 600
    600 people were at the concert.

17.
    ```
    pencils  [    |    |    ]  ⎫
                              ⎬ 150
    pens     [    |    ]       ⎭
             ?
    ```

    5 units → 150
    1 unit → 150 ÷ 5 = 30
    2 units → 2 × 30 = 60 pens
    5 units → 60 ÷ 5 = 12
    4 units → 4 × 12 = 48 rulers
    There are **48** rulers.

18. (a) Simone:Her sister
       4:5
   The ratio of Simone's age to her sister's age is **4:5**.

   (b) $\dfrac{\text{Her sister's age}}{\text{Total age}} = \dfrac{5}{4+5} = \dfrac{5}{9}$

   Her sister's age is $\dfrac{5}{9}$ of the total age of both girls.

19.   5 − 3 units → 40 in.
          2 units → 40 in.
           1 unit → 40 ÷ 2 = 20 in.
       3 + 4 + 5 units → 12 × 20 cm = 240 in.
   The perimeter of the triangle is **240 in.**

20.   5 − 3 units → 30
        2 units → 30
         1 unit → 30 ÷ 2 = 15
         8 units → 8 × 15 = 120
   Anita has 120 oranges and lemons altogether.
   5 units → 120
   1 unit → 120 ÷ 5 = 24
   7 units → 7 × 24 = 168
   Winnie has **168** oranges and lemons altogether.

21. (a)   Lulu:Isaac   Isaac:Amanda
       $4 \times \left(\begin{array}{c}3:7\\12:28\end{array}\right) \times 4$ $7 \times \left(\begin{array}{c}4:3\\28:21\end{array}\right) \times 7$

       21 − 12 units → $45
         9 units → $45
          1 unit → $45 ÷ 9 = $5
         28 units → 28 × $5 = $140
       Isaac has **$140**.

   (b) 12 + 28 + 21 = 61
       61 × $5 = $305
       The three children have **$305** altogether.

22. 30 × 28 × 20 = 16,800 cm³
   The volume of the rectangular metal block is 16,800 cm³.
   7 + 3 units → 16,800 cm³
    1 unit → 16,800 ÷ 10 = 1,680 cm³
    7 units → 1,680 × 7 = 11,760 cm³
    3 units → 1,680 × 3 = 5,040 cm³
   11,760 × 7.6 g = 89,376 g
   5,040 × 6.5 g = 32,760 g
   89,376 + 32,760 = 122,136 g = 122.136 kg ≈ 122 kg
   The mass of the metal block is **122 kg**.

23. 64 − 24 + 30 = 70
   There were 70 boys and girls at the party in the end.
   2 + 5 units → 70
    7 units → 70
     1 unit → 70 ÷ 7 = 10
     2 units → 2 × 10 = 20
   20 + 24 = 44
   There were **44** boys at first

24.

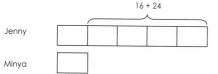

4 units → 16 + 24 = 40
1 unit → 40 ÷ 4 = 10
10 + 16 + 16 = 42
Jenny had **42** stickers at first.

25. Before

   After

   10 + 20 + 20 + 10 = 60
   2 × 60 = 120
   Arthur had **120** postcards in the end.

26. (a) purple:total
        5:5 + 4
        5:9
   The ratio of the pieces of purple-colored paper to the total pieces of paper Aaron uses for each brochure is **5:9**.

   (b) 320 × 4 = 1280
       The total pieces of cream-colored paper he uses is **1,280**.

27. (a) turkey:ham   turkey:ham
       $2 \times \left(\begin{array}{c}7:3\\14:6\end{array}\right) \times 2$ $3 \times \left(\begin{array}{c}3:2\\9:6\end{array}\right) \times 3$

       14 − 9 units → 15 lb.
         5 units → 15 lb.
          1 unit → 15 ÷ 5 = 3 lb.
         14 units → 14 × 3 = 42
       The deli had **42 lb.** of turkey in the morning.

   (b) 6 × 3 = 18
       The deli had **18 lb.** of ham in the morning.

28. 6 + 5 units → 33
    11 units → 33
     1 unit → 33 ÷ 11 = 3
     9 units → 9 × 3 = 27
   Alfonso swam **27** laps on the second day of the swimming lesson.

29. (a) sugar:flour   butter:sugar
       $2 \times \left(\begin{array}{c}3:5\\6:10\end{array}\right) \times 2$ 5:6

       Total: 6 + 10 + 5 = 21
       The ratio of the mass of sugar used to the mass of flour used to the total mass of the three ingredients was **6:10:21**.

   (b) 10 − 6 units → 100 g
         4 units → 100 g
          1 unit → 100 ÷ 4 = 25 g
         5 units → 5 × 25 = 125 g
       She used **125 g** of butter to bake a cake.

30. (a) $\dfrac{\text{elbow macaroni}}{\text{pasta shells}} = \dfrac{100}{300} = \dfrac{1}{3}$
       The amount of elbow macaroni is $\dfrac{1}{3}$ the amount of pasta shells.

Singapore Math Practice Level 6A

(b)   5 units → 100 + 300 = 400 g
       1 unit → 400 ÷ 5 = 80 g
       35 units → 35 × 80 = 2,800 g
       She needs **2,800 g** of pasta shells and elbow macaroni altogether.

Unit 6: Percentage

1. **80%**

   $\frac{4}{5} \times 100 = 80\%$

2. **13%**

   $\frac{13}{100} \times 100 = 13\%$

3. **2%**

   $\frac{8}{400} \times 100 = 2\%$

4. **16.8%**

   $\frac{42}{250} \times 100 = 16.8\%$

5. **34%**

   $\frac{17^{\times 2}}{50_{\times 2}} = \frac{34}{100} = 34\%$

6. **5%**

   $\frac{1^{\times 5}}{20_{\times 5}} = \frac{5}{100} = 5\%$

7. **64%**

   $\frac{16^{\times 4}}{25_{\times 4}} = \frac{64}{100} = 64\%$

8. **12%**

   $\frac{96^{\div 8}}{800_{\div 8}} = \frac{12}{100} = 12\%$

9. **60%**

   $\frac{216}{360} \times 100 = 60\%$

10. **45%**

    $\frac{405}{900} \times 100 = 45\%$

11. **68%**

    $0.68 \times 100 = 68\%$

12. **7%**

    $0.07 \times 100 = 7\%$

13. **21.5%**

    $0.215 \times 100 = 21.5\%$

14. **80.4%**

    $0.804 \times 100 = 80.4\%$

15. **30%**

    $0.3 \times 100 = 30\%$

16. $\frac{12}{25}$

    $48\% = \frac{48}{100} = \frac{12}{25}$

17. $\frac{9}{100}$

    $9\% = \frac{9}{100}$

18. $\frac{3}{20}$

    $15\% = \frac{15}{100} = \frac{3}{20}$

19. $\frac{1}{500}$

    $0.2\% = 0.2 \div 100 = 0.002$

    $0.002 = \frac{2}{1000} = \frac{1}{500}$

20. $\frac{49}{50}$

    $98\% = \frac{98}{100} = \frac{49}{50}$

21. **0.73**

    $73\% = 73 \div 100 = 0.73$

22. **0.68**

    $68\% = 68 \div 100 = 0.68$

23. **0.84**

    $84\% = 84 \div 100 = 0.84$

24. **0.03**

    $3\% = 3 \div 100 = 0.03$

25. **0.07**

    $7\% = 7 \div 100 = 0.07$

26. **25%**

    $35 - \$28 = \$7$

    $\frac{7}{28} \times 100\% = 25\%$

27. **25%**

    $\frac{750}{3,000} \times 100\% = 25\%$

28. **20%**

    $\frac{240}{1,200} \times 100\% = 20\%$

29. **180 blue marbles**

    $100\% - 25\% - 15\% = 60\%$

    $\frac{60}{100} \times 300 = 180$

30. **$126.50**

    $100\% - 45\% = 55\%$

    $\frac{55}{100} \times \$230 = \$126.50$

31. **13 students**

    $100\% - 35\% = 65\%$

    $\frac{65}{100} \times 40 = 26$

    $26 \div 2 = 13$

32. **162 female adults**

    $100\% - 48\% - 25\% = 27\%$

    $\frac{27}{100} \times 600 = 162$

33. **$38.40**

    $100\% - 20\% = 80\%$

    $100\% \to \$48$

    $80\% \to \frac{\$48}{100} \times 80 = \$38.40$

34. **$1,840**

    $100\% + 15\% = 115\%$

    $100\% \to \$1,600$

    $115\% \to \frac{\$1,600}{100} \times 115 = \$1,840$

35. **$45**

    $100\% + 7\% \to \$48.15$

    $100\% \to \frac{\$48.15}{107} \times 100 = \$45$

Singapore Math Practice Level 6A

36. **$408**

$\frac{4}{100} \times \$10,200 = \$408$

37. **20%**

$45 - \$36 = \$9$

$45 \to 100\%$

$\$1 \to \frac{100}{45}\%$

$\$9 \to 9 \times \frac{100}{45}\% = 20\%$

38. **12.5%**

$63 - 56 = 7$ kg

$56 \to 100\%$

$1 \to \frac{100}{56}\%$

$7 \to 7 \times \frac{100}{56} = 12.5\%$

39. **20%**

$1,200 - 720 = 480$ girls

$\frac{720}{1,200} \times 100\% = 60\%$

$100\% - 60\% = 40\%$

$60\% - 40\% = 20\%$

40. **28%**

$100\% - 20\% = 80\%$

$80\% \to \$2,640$

$1\% \to \frac{\$2,640}{80} = \$33$

$100\% \to \$33 \times 100 = \$3,300$

The original price of the diamond ring was $3,300.

$\frac{924}{3,300} \times 100 = 28\%$

41. $299 + \$148 = \$447$

Both items cost $447 before the 7% sales tax.

$100\% \to \$447$

$100\% + 7\% \to \frac{\$447}{100} \times 107 = \$478.29$

He would pay **$478.29** in all if both items were subjected to a 7% sales tax.

42. $100\% - 30\% = 70\%$

$100\% + 70\% = 170\%$

$170\% \to 153$

$1\% \to \frac{153}{170}$

$100\% \to 100 \times \frac{153}{170} = 90$

Manuel has **90** marbles.

43. $100\% - 30\% - 14\% = 56\%$

$56\% \to \$160 + \$120 = \$280$

$1\% \to \frac{\$280}{56} = \$5$

$100\% \to 100 \times \$5 = \$500$

Rebecca's weekly salary was **$500**.

44. $\frac{40}{100} \times 790 = 316$

$790 + 316 = 1,106$

The number of children enrolled in summer camp in 2008 was 1,106.

$790 + 1,106 = 1,896$

The number of students enrolled in the enrichment camp in these two years was **1,896**.

45. $100\% - 65\% = 35\%$

$35\% \to \$1,609.65$

$1\% \to \frac{\$1,609.65}{35} = \$45.99$

$100\% \to 100 \times \$45.99 = \$4,599$

The original price of the leather sofa was **$4,599**.

46. (a) $18 \times 6 = 108$

$45\% \to 108$

$1\% \to \frac{108}{45}$

$20\% \to \frac{108}{45} \times 20 = 48$

She completed **48** worksheets on the first day.

(b) $48 + 108 = 156$

Marisol did **156** worksheets altogether.

47. $3,099 - \$2,135 = \$964$

$\frac{964}{3,099} \times 100\% = 31.11\% \approx 31\%$

The percentage decrease in price was **31%**.

48. $100\% - 25\% = 75\%$

$\frac{3}{5} \times 75\% = 45\%$

He donated 45% of his money to the charity.

$100\% - 25\% - 45\% = 30\%$

$30\% \to \$4,200$

$1\% \to \frac{\$4,200}{30} = \$140$

$25\% \to 25 \times \$140 = \$3,500$

He gave **$3,500** to his wife.

49. (a) $5,075 - \$5,000 = \$75$

$\frac{\$75}{\$5,000} \times 100\% = 1.5\%$

The interest rate on the money Jong deposited was **1.5%**.

(b) $1.5\% \times \$5,075 = \$76.125$

$5,075 + \$76.125 = \$5,151.125 \approx \$5,151.13$

He would get **$5,151.13** in all if he decided to close his savings account after the second year.

50. (a) $100\% + 7\% = 107\%$

$107\% \to \$627.02$

$1\% \to \$627.02 \div 107 = \$5.86$

$7\% \to 7 \times \$5.86 = \$41.02$

Mr. López paid **$41.02** for the sales tax.

(b) $627.02 - \$41.02 = \$586$

$586 \div 8 = \$73.25$

Each person paid **$73.25**.

Review 3

1. **(1)**

$39\% = 39 \div 100 = 0.39$

2. **(4)**

$\frac{3}{5}\frac{\times 20}{\times 20} = \frac{60}{100} = 60\%$

3. **(1)**
20 − 12 = 8
There are 8 girls.
girls:boys
8:12
2:3

4. **(4)**
length:width
$5 \times \left(\begin{array}{c} 5:8 \\ 25:40 \end{array} \right) \times 5$
25 + 40 + 25 + 40 = 130 in.

5. **(3)**
100% − 45% − 30% = 25%
30% − 25% → $210
5% → $210
1% → $210 ÷ 5 = $42
45% → 45 × $42 = $1,890

6. **(3)**
8 + 7 units → 675
1 unit → 675 ÷ 15 = 45
7 units → 7 × 45 = 315

7. **(2)**
100% − 20% → $42
80% → $42
$1\% \rightarrow \dfrac{\$42}{80} = \$0.525$
20% → $0.525 × 20 = $10.50

8. $\dfrac{6}{25}$

$\dfrac{24}{100} = \dfrac{6}{25}$

9. **29 : 16**
7 + 3 units → 90
1 unit → 90 ÷ 10 = 9
7 units → 7 × 9 = 63
3 units → 3 × 9 = 27
63 − 5 = 58
27 + 5 = 32
Tim:Lisa
58:32
29:16

10. **$208.80**
$\dfrac{42}{100} \times \$360 = \$151.20$
$360 − $151.20 = $208.80

11. **$75**
100% + 10% = 110%
110% → $82.50
$1\% \rightarrow \dfrac{\$82.50}{110} = \$0.75$
100% → 100 × $0.75 = $75

12. **29 years old**
Bobby:Eileen
$3 \times \left(\begin{array}{c} 7:6 \\ 21:18 \end{array} \right) \times 3$
21 + 8 = 29

13. **600 French books**

100% − 39% − 25% − 16% = 20%
$\dfrac{20}{100} \times 3{,}000 = 600$

14. **27 more raisins**
8 units → 72
1 unit → 72 ÷ 8 = 9
8 − 5 = 3 units
3 units → 3 × 9 = 27

15. **$2,484**
5 units → $540
1 unit → $540 ÷ 5 = $108
7 + 5 + 11 = 23 units
23 units → 23 × $108 = $2484

16. 3 + 5 = 8 units
8 units → 600
1 unit → 600 ÷ 8 = 75
3 units → 3 × 75 = 225 blue beads
5 units → 5 × 75 = 375 red beads
225 − 49 = 176 blue beads
375 − 243 = 132 red beads
blue:red
176:132
4:3
The new ratio of the number of blue beads to the number of red beads is **4:3**.

17. Xavier → 100%
Yolanda → $\dfrac{40}{100} \times 100\% = 40\%$
40% + 100% = 140%
Zara → $\dfrac{60}{100} \times 140\% = 84\%$
84% → $1,176
1% → $1,176 ÷ 84 = $14
100% + 140% + 84% = 324%
324% × $14 = $4,536
The sum of money was **$4,536**.

18. 100% − 15% − 34% = 51%
51% − 15% → 720 g
36% → 720 g
$1\% \rightarrow \dfrac{720}{36} = 20$ g
100% → 100 × 20 = 2,000 g
Sandra had **2,000 g** of flour at first.

19. $27 000 ÷ 6 = $4500
Fina's monthly salary is $4,500.
$\dfrac{25}{100} \times \$4{,}500 = \$1{,}125$
$4,500 + $1,125 = $5,625
Corrine's monthly salary is $5,625.
12 × $5,625 = $67,500
Corrine's annual salary is **$67,500**.

20. (a) cars:motorcycles:trucks
$5_{\times 2}{:}4_{\times 2}$
8:5
10:8:5
10 + 8 units → 1,044
18 units → 1,044
1 unit → 1,044 ÷ 18 = 58

Singapore Math Practice Level 6A

8 – 5 = 3 units
3 units → 58 × 3 = 174
There are **174** more motorcycles than trucks.
(b) 10 + 8 + 5 = 23
58 × 23 = 1334
There are **1,334** vehicles on the road during rush hour.

Final Review

1. **(3)**
2. **(3)**
    $0.8\overset{\frown}{7} \times 100 = 87$
3. **(1)**
    4 m 5 cm = 400 cm + 5 cm = 405 cm
4. **(2)**
    37 – 9 = 28
    28 ÷ 2 = 14 female students
    14 + 9 = 23 male students
    $\dfrac{\text{male students}}{\text{total students}} = \dfrac{23}{37}$
5. **(4)**
    $2 + \dfrac{3^{\times 25}}{4_{\times 25}} = 2 + \dfrac{75}{100} = 2 + 0.75 = 2.75$
6. **(3)**
    0.811 m × 100 = 81.1 cm
    81.1 cm ≈ 81 cm
7. **(3)**
    ∠ABD = 180° – 90° – 42°
    $\quad$ = 48° (∠s on a straight line)
    ∠h = 180° – 90° – 48° = 42° (sum of ∠s in a Δ = 180°)
8. **(3)**
    6 units → 36x
    1 unit → 36x ÷ 6 = 6x
    6x + 36x + 6x + 36x = 84x
9. **(2)**
    4 × 7 = 28
    The total of the four numbers is 28.
    28 + 12 = 40
    40 ÷ 5 = 8
10. **(1)**
    100% + 15% → $2,300
    $\qquad$ 115% → $2,300
    $\qquad\quad$ 1% → $\dfrac{\$2,300}{115}$ = $20
    $\qquad$ 100% → 100 × $20 = $2,000
11. **(2)**
    $9.50 + $0.65 = $10.15
    $10.15 – $7 = $3.15
    $3.15 + $3.80 = $6.95
12. **(3)**
    $8 \div \dfrac{4}{5} = 8^{2} \times \dfrac{5}{\cancel{4}_{1}} = 10$
13. **(2)**
    (5 × $48) + (2 × $70) = $240 + $140 = $380
14. **(2)**

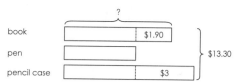

$13.30 – $1.90 – $3 = $8.40
$8.40 ÷ 3 = $2.80
$2.80 + $1.90 = $4.70
15. **(2)**
    100% – 25% = 75%
    75% → $150
    $\quad$ 1% → $\dfrac{\$150}{75}$ = $2
    25% → 25 × $2 = $50
16. **180°**
    ∠z = ∠ACB
    ∠x + ∠y + ∠z = 180° (sum of ∠s in a Δ = 180°)
17. $\dfrac{3}{8}$
    $2\dfrac{1}{8} - 1\dfrac{3}{4} = 2\dfrac{1}{8} - 1\dfrac{6}{8} = 1\dfrac{9}{8} - 1\dfrac{6}{8} = \dfrac{3}{8}$
18.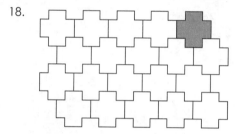
19. **$255**
    100% → $300
    $\quad$ 1% → $300 ÷ 100 = $3
    100% – 15% = 85%
    $\quad$ 85% → 85 × $3 = $255
20. **$21**
    4 × $96 = $384
    $426 – $384 = $42
    $42 ÷ 2 = $21
21.
22. **2 gal.**
    5 gal. – 3 gal. = 2 gal.
23. **35 km**
    From the graph, the van traveled 35 mi. with 5 gal. of gasoline.
24. **7 mi.**
    35 ÷ 5 = 7 mi.
25. **84°**
26. **5**
    $\dfrac{6y + 4y + 5}{11} = \dfrac{(6 \times 5) + (4 \times 5) + 5}{11} = \dfrac{55}{11} = 5$
27. **3 P.M.**
    Quarter past two is 2:15 P.M.

28. **28.82**
28 ones 8 tenths 2 hundredths = 28.82

29. **24:6:1**

A :B	B:C	A:B:C
$4_{×6}:1_{×6}$	6:1	24:6:1

30. **8,080 in.²**
Area of the rectangle = 124 × 80 = 9,920 in.²
124 – 28 – 78 = 18 in.
Area of the smaller triangle = $\frac{1}{2}$ × 18 × 80 = 720 in.²
Area of the bigger triangle = $\frac{1}{2}$ × 28 × 80 = 1,120 in.²
9,920 – 1,120 – 720 = 8,080 in.²

31. **2**
$\frac{1}{8} + \frac{3}{8} = \frac{4}{8}$
$\frac{4}{8} ÷ \frac{1}{4} = \frac{4}{8_2} × \frac{4^1}{1} = \frac{4}{2} = 2$

32. **145°**
∠DBC = 180° – 150° = 30°   (∠s on a straight line)
∠BDC = 180° – 65° = 115°   (∠s on a straight line)
∠BCD = 180° – 30° – 115° = 35° (sum of ∠s in a △ = 180°)
∠a = 180° – 35° = 145°

33. **65 cm**
3 m 25 cm = 300 cm + 25 cm = 325 cm
$\frac{20}{100}$ × 325 = 65 cm

34. **$22.25**
3 × $9.25 = $27.75
$50 – $27.75 = $22.25

35. **21 kg**
60 × 325 g = 19 500 g = 19.5 kg
19.5 kg + 1.44 kg = 20.94 kg ≈ 21 kg

36. 45 + 50 = 95
There are 95 staff in the chain of restaurants.
$\frac{60}{100}$ × 95 = 57
57 of them are new staff.
95 – 57 = 38
$\frac{50}{100}$ × 38 = 19
There are **19** permanent staff.

37. Fare for the first mile = $2.50
    5 mi. = $\frac{1}{4}$x
(4) 5 = $\frac{1}{4}$x (4)
20 = x
20 × $0.40 = $8.00
Fare for the next 5 mi. = $8.00
7.8 mi. – 6 mi. = 1.8 mi.
1.8 = $\frac{1}{10}$x
(10)1.8 = $\frac{1}{10}$x (10)
18 = x

18 × $0.20 = $3.60
Fare for the last 1.8 mi. = $3.60
$2.50 + $8.00 + $3.60 = $14.10
Rieko would have to pay **$14.10** if she traveled 7.8 mi.

38. (a) 8 × 15y = 120y
There were 120y apples in all.
120y – 8y – 17 = 112y – 17
He had **(112y – 17)** apples left.

    (b) 112y – 17 = (112 × 20) – 17
                    = 2,223
He had **2,223** apples left.

39.

		86	
Lenny	?	22	64
Bob	?	22	

86 – 22 = 64
64 – 22 = 42
Each of them received 42 marbles from Emilio.
2 × 42 = 84
Emilio gave **84** marbles to both of them.

40. $1 - \frac{5}{8} = \frac{3}{8}$
$\frac{2}{3} × \frac{3}{8} = \frac{1}{4}$
Eliza received $\frac{1}{4}$ of the money.
$1 - \frac{5}{8} - \frac{1}{4} = \frac{1}{8}$
Vicky received $\frac{1}{8}$ of the money.
$\frac{5}{8} - \frac{1}{8} = \frac{4}{8}$
Claire received $\frac{4}{8}$ of the money more than Vicky.
$\frac{4}{8} × \$90 = \$45$
Claire received **$45** more than Vicky.

41. 28% + 7% = 35%
35% of the participants were fifth graders.
100% – 35% – 28% = 37%
37% of the participants were sixth graders.
35% + 28% = 63%
63% – 37% → 910
    26% → 910
     1% → $\frac{910}{26}$ = 35
    37% → 37 × 35 = 1,295
1,295 sixth graders attended the assembly.

42. (a) 2 × 65.2 = 130.4 kg
130.4 – 62.3 = 68.1 kg
Harry's mass is 68.1 kg.
2 × 58.6 = 117.2 kg
117.2 – 62.3 = 54.9 kg
Charlie's mass is 54.9 kg.
68.1 + 54.9 = 123 kg
123 ÷ 2 = 61.5 kg
The average mass of Harry and Charlie is **61.5 kg**.

    (b) 68.1 + 54.9 + 62.3 = 185.3 kg
The total mass of the three boys is **185.3 kg**.

43. (a) $4 \times 9 = 36$ yd.

The perimeter of the square field is 36 yd.

square field:rectangular field

$$12 \times \left(\begin{matrix} 3:2 \\ 36:24 \end{matrix} \right) \times 12$$

The perimeter of the rectangular field is **24 yd.**

(b) $24 - 8 - 8 = 8$ m

$8 \div 2 = 4$ m

The width of the rectangular field is **4 m.**

44. $25\% = \frac{25}{100} = \frac{1}{4}$

$\frac{1}{4}$ of Donna's coins were quarters.

$1 - \frac{3}{5} - \frac{1}{4} = \frac{3}{20}$

$\frac{3}{20}$ of Donna's coins were dimes.

$\$20 \div \$0.25 = 80$

There were 80 quarters.

$\frac{1}{4} = \frac{5}{20} \rightarrow 80$ coins

$\frac{1}{20} \rightarrow 80 \div 5 = 16$ coins

$\frac{3}{20} \rightarrow 16 \times 3 = 48$ coins

There were 48 dimes.

$\frac{3}{5} = \frac{12}{20} \rightarrow 12 \times 16 = 192$ nickels

There were 192 nickels.

$(192 \times \$0.05) + (80 \times \$0.25) + (48 \times \$0.10) = \$34.40$

The total amount of money Donna had was **$34.40.**

45. (a) $\frac{2}{5} \times \$375 = \$150$

Mrs. Anderson pays **$150** for her cell phone every month.

(b) $1 - \frac{1}{5} = \frac{4}{5}$

$\frac{4}{5} \times \$375 = \$300$

Mr. Anderson pays **$300** for his cell phone in the following month.

$1 - \frac{1}{6} = \frac{5}{6}$

$\frac{5}{6} \times \$150 = \$125$

Mrs. Anderson pays $125 for her mobile bill in the following month.

$\$300 + \$125 = \$425$

Both of them pay **$425** for their mobile bills in the following month.

46. $\frac{2}{3} \times 600 = 400$

There are 400 men.

$600 - 400 = 200$

There are 200 women and children.

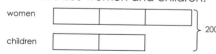

$200 \div 5 = 40$

$3 \times 40 = 120$

There are 120 women.

$200 - 120 = 80$

There are 80 children.

$1 - \frac{1}{10} = \frac{9}{10}$

$\frac{9}{10} \times 120 = 108$

108 women can swim.

$1 - \frac{1}{4} = \frac{3}{4}$

$\frac{3}{4} \times 80 = 60$

60 children can swim.

47. (a) $\frac{1}{2} \rightarrow 630$ g

$1 \rightarrow 2 \times 630 = 1260$ g $= 1.26$ kg

The jar can hold **1.26 kg** of cookies when it is full.

(b) $\frac{7}{9} - \frac{1}{2} \rightarrow 855 - 630$

$\frac{5}{18} \rightarrow 225$ g

$\frac{1}{18} \rightarrow 225 \div 5 = 45$ g

$\frac{18}{18} \rightarrow 18 \times 45 = 810$ g

The mass of the cookies is 810 g.

$1,260 - 810 = 450$ g

The mass of the empty jar is **450 g.**

48. (a) $\$18 - \$3 = \$15$

Each picture frame cost $15.

$(4 \times \$15) + (3 \times \$18) = \$114$

For every 4 picture frames and 3 albums, Marie paid $114.

$\$1,026 \div \$114 = 9$

$9 \times 4 = 36$ picture frames

$9 \times 3 = 27$ albums

She bought **27** albums and **36** picture frames in all.

(b) $36 \times \$15 = \$540$

$\$540 \div \$18 = 30$

If Marie did not buy any picture frames, she could buy **30** more albums with the same amount of money.

Challenge Questions

1.

Box A	100%	70%	
Box B	100%		
Box C	100%	70%	100%	70%

$\Big\}$ 244

$100\% + 70\% + 100\% +$
$100\% + 70\% + 100\% + 70\% \rightarrow 244$
$610\% \rightarrow 244$
$1\% \rightarrow 244 \div 610 = 0.4$

$170\% \times 0.4 = 68$

There were **68** pencils in box A.

$100\% \times 0.4 = 40$

There were **40** pencils in box B.

$68 \times 2 = 136$

There were **136** pencils in box C.

Singapore Math Practice Level 6A

2. $1000 – $890 = $110

$110 → 110 × 99 = 10,890 Japanese yen

She exchanged the remaining dollars for 10,890 Japanese yen.

10,890 – 10,000 = 890

890 Japanese yen → $\frac{890}{133}$ × 0.75 = 5.018

$$≈ 5 \text{ Euros}$$

She exchanged the remaining Japanese yen for **5 Euros**.

3. 90 + 80 – 70 – 60 + 50 – 40 – 30 = 20

4. 76 – 50 = 26

The team got 26 points for answering 25 questions.

(25 × 2) – 26 = 24

The team had lost 24 points for not answering all 25 questions correctly.

2 + 1 = 3

3 points were lost for not answering a question correctly.

24 ÷ 3 = 8

It got **8** questions wrong.

5.
13	2	12	7	34
5	3	11	15	34
8	4	6	16	34
14	1	10	9	34

13 + 2 + 12 + 7 = 34

5 + 3 + 11 + 15 = 34

8 + 4 + 6 + 16 = 34

14 + 1 + 10 + 9 = 34

6. Since all their digits add up to 34,

34 ÷ 2 = 17

The sum of the two digits is 17.

To add up to 17, there are only digits 8 and 9.

89 + 98 = 187

X and Y are **89** and **98**.

7. 500,000 ÷ 99 = $5,050.51

He exchanged 500,000 Japanese yen for $5,050.51.

$5,050.51 ÷ 2 = $2,525.26

$2,525.26 × 13.79 = 34,823.34

$$≈ 34,823$$

He sent home **34,823** pesos.

8. Use the Guess-and-Check method.

80 × 81 = 6,480   [too high]

70 × 71 = 4,970   [high]

60 × 61 = 3,660   [too low]

The page numbers must be between 60 and 70.

63 × 64 = 4,032

The page numbers were **63** and **64**.

9. 100% + 15% = 115% → $5,290

1% → $5,290 ÷ 115 = $46

100% → $46 × 100 = $4,600

His monthly pay in year 2008 was $4,600.

115% → $4600

1% → $4600 ÷ 115 = $40

100% → $40 × 100 = $4,000

His monthly pay in year 2006 was **$4,000**.

10. 29 + 28 + 27 + 26 + 25 + 24 + 23 + 22 + 21 + 20 + 19 + 18 + 17 + 16 + 15 + 14 + 13 + 12 + 11 + 10 + 9 + 8 + 7 + 6 + 5 + 4 + 3 + 2 + 1 = 435

435 handshakes were exchanged.

11.
```
    ×2    ×2    ×2    ×2    ×2    ×2    ×2
23,  46,  92,  184,  368,  736,  1472,  2944
```
The pattern is multiplying the preceding numbers by 2.

12.
8	9	1
7	4	3
6	2	5

12 × 6 = 72

14 × 6 = 84

10 × 6 = 60

8 × 9 × 1 = 72

7 × 4 × 3 = 84

6 × 2 × 5 = 60

Singapore Math Practice Level 6A